MARGARET RANDALL

FIRST

LAUGH

ESSAYS, 2000–2009

University of Nebraska Press / Lincoln and London

An abridged version of "Can Poetry Matter?" first appeared in *World Literature Today* 84.2 (March–April 2010): 20–22, and is reprinted here by permission.

A complete version of "Can Poetry Matter?" appeared in *Mandorla* 13 (2010).

Set in Electra by Kim Essman. Designed by Nathan Putens.

Library of Congress Cataloging-in-Publication Data
Randall, Margaret, 1936–
First laugh : essays, 2000–2009 / Margaret Randall.
p. cm.   "Four of these essays are based on talks given in different places and on different subjects. The rest are new and unpublished"—P. .
Includes bibliographical references.
ISBN 978-0-8032-3477-2 (paperback : alkaline paper)
1. United States—Social conditions.
2. Latin America—Social conditions.
3. Poetry—Social aspects. 4. Feminist criticism. 5. Randall, Margaret, 1936– —Political and social views. I. Title.
II. Title: Essays, 2000–2009.
HN57.R26 2011
306.0973—dc22   2010026443

For my granddaughter,
Lía Margarita Randall Carlevaro

CONTENTS

A Few Words
about These Essays

More than half these musings were written during the tumul-
tuous years between 2006 and 2009. At first the country and
world were immersed in what felt like a last-gasp attempt to
throw off the stifling death culture personified by George W.
Bush. Were we going to let him take us all down? Would his
lies, pomposity, overheating climate, criminal disregard for
resources, preemptive strikes, invasions of sovereign nations,
crass anti-intellectualism, and contempt for science and art be
the last policy blunders anyone knew?

Everywhere people were fighting back, but these struggles
were uneven and more often than not resulted in frustration.
Following 9/11, when the administration announced we were
engaged in a war against terrorism, an effective anti-war move-

ment never completely coalesced. Inadequate health care and faltering public education provoked outrage and some organizing efforts, but catchy phrases such as "No Child Left Behind"—language put forth to confuse—made it seem to many as if the important problems were being addressed. The economy still appeared to be good; few realized it was a bubble about to burst.

Hundreds of thousands of mostly young people were attending yearly World Social Forums and protesting international trade that favored wealthy nations at the expense of the poor, and workers in those nations at the expense of the owner class. China, already the world's fastest-growing economy, would soon rival the United States as a global power, yet half a century had not diminished the Tibetan people's struggle for the return of their homeland. Africans were battling generations of international aid mentality as they turned to their own cultural traditions for more effective ways of addressing dramatic social injustice. Radical groups (called terrorist here) had won democratic elections in Lebanon and Palestine; and the Palestinians, against enormous odds, had not given up on reclaiming their territory.

As Bush kept his eyes on the Middle East, a range of progressive governments emerged across Latin America: from Venezuela's Chávez to the FLMN's stunning victory in El Salvador, and including Brazil, Bolivia, Chile, Uruguay, Argentina, and Paraguay. Mexico had come close, and the Zapatistas in the southern part of that country were redefining power. Cuba, with all its contradictions, still stood proud ninety miles from U.S. shores. These governments vary in their positions, from liberal to extreme left, but they have been able to constitute a bloc capable of standing up to U.S. coercion and interference.

Throughout the world, people's psychological need to make

peace with historical atrocities was producing a series of power-ful truth and reconciliation commissions: beginning with South Africa's public coming to terms with apartheid and including experiences of different sorts in Chile, Argentina, Germany, Peru, Sierra Leone, Morocco, and elsewhere. In Peru, ex-president Alberto Fujimori was tried and convicted of crimes that sent him to prison for what may well be the rest of his life. Memo-rializing history, aided by a new technology of memory, and each of these national calls to accountability, amnesty, and/or restitution—whatever their scope or outcome—helped heal our wounded humanity in some important way.

Here in the United States, as 2007 became 2008, the two Democratic front-runners for president of a still sexist, still rac-ist nation were a white woman and an African American man. Only a couple of years before, we would not have believed it possible. Great numbers of women supported Hillary Clinton. A new generation of young people, many with little prior involve-ment in electoral politics, rallied around Barack Obama. The movement for change swept the country with such energy that even the conservative Right was forced to present a female vice-presidential candidate (crassly symbolic as she turned out to be). On November 4, 2008, Obama became the first U.S. president-elect of color. Not only here but throughout the world, expectations ran high.

Suddenly Bush was out, Obama in. But change isn't easy, and even the best intentions are complicated by entrenched power and a culture of governmental quid pro quo. The new president, brilliant and articulate as he is, faces problems easier to attack during a campaign than to solve once in office. Each of us, from wherever we stand on the political spectrum, has had to adjust our expectations. It is a lesson in the overarching mechanisms of a system as opposed to the efforts of individuals, no matter how concerned or sincere. For many it may also have been the last time they will believe that "change is possible."

My own political coming of age began in the chilly wake of McCarthyism, within the context of the civil rights and mid-twentieth-century women's movements, shaped by a seemingly endless war in Southeast Asia, and while living and working in three Latin American countries: Mexico, Cuba, and Nicaragua. For three decades I was privileged to live, raise my four children, and work in an atmosphere of hope. And so, for me, like so many leftists of my generation, the implosion of European socialism in 1989–90 was more than a political setback; it was a strike at our very identities. Would we ever be able to extricate ourselves from such multilayered defeat?

In my case personal change accompanied political change. The two have long been inextricably linked for me. Elsewhere I have written about the immigration case I was forced to fight upon my return to my country of origin in 1984, about coming out as a lesbian in midlife after several long-term relationships with men, and about the discovery of incest in my earliest childhood (leading to a deep interest in cellular memory and its impact on our lives, examined here in "The Cell Remembers"). A changing political scene didn't change my core values or writing interests. But experience broadened them, and age did alter the way I began to write about the issues that continue to concern me. I returned to an early fascination with language armed with a more nuanced perception and deepened need for connection.

In important ways the essays in *First Laugh* are an extension, and perhaps a more targeted exploration, of these ongoing concerns. Their precision, form, and style are noticeably different from what I have written up to now. In general they are shorter. I need fewer words to say what I want to say. Rather than launch more involved expositions, with an abundance of statistical data and reasoned analysis, these pieces are most often rooted in a tangible moment or event and move out from there, focusing on feeling and only occasionally backed up by a lot of data. I may start obsessing about something like the earliest human laughter and track it until I am exhausted by its implications ("First Laugh") or ponder the walls that divide us and imagine how their structures might be dismantled ("Piercing the Walls").

Four of these essays are based on talks given in different places and on different subjects. The rest are new and unpublished. The most recent, which make up about 60 percent of the collection, were also written using a very different methodology. While I used to get an idea, start writing, and make my way through to the end—with rewrites of course—these began with an idea that would then become a paragraph or page, and I'd find myself adding pieces here and there, inserting them wherever they seemed to fit, much like building a piece of sculpture, adding squares to a quilt, or fitting together the pieces of a complex puzzle. Their construction necessarily shapes their structure and tone. They verge on personal narrative.

I wonder if it is age that has so changed my writing style. In my mid-seventies I find I am much more interested in making connections than in developing an idea from beginning to end. And the connections may come to me in the middle of the night, during a walk to my favorite café, or in epistolary or face-to-face conversation with one of the number of fecund minds I am privileged to have in my life.

Memory, or its failure, plays a role in this. As I write I often forget a word or phrase. I may see its color (my life with *synesthesia* is addressed in several of these essays, most notably "Pumping Gas" and "The Place Where Color Sounds") even as language resists. I've developed a wild patience as I wait for a word to reappear,[1] but I've also noticed that my whole thought process has shifted, such that I find myself writing from the center out rather than from beginning to end. I do not believe these changes denote a lessening of creative power, just the opposite. Age, so far, has brought me a sharper ability to strengthen the bridge I have been building throughout my creative life.

Even as forgetting takes up residence within, the language becomes more important. It moves in and settles in the spaces left by memory loss. Words, when remembered, explode in prisms of meaning, energy, tone, hue. Strings of words move like newly discovered byways across old maps. These texts explore language itself: how it is used by others and how I choose to use it.

I have referred to fecund minds and would like to acknowledge some of them here. Several belong to my grandchildren; with love and gratitude I dedicate this book to the oldest of these: my namesake, Lía Margarita. Some belong to my children: Gregory, Sarah, Ximena, and Ana. I am so proud of each, and what they are doing with their lives. Some belong to friends whose warmth, wisdom, and curiosity have enriched me for many years: among these, in the context of this particular book, are Susan Sherman, Jane Norling, Robert Schweitzer, Roxanne Dunbar-Ortíz, Ruth Salvaggio, and my brother, John Randall. The mind that is closest, in identification as well as proximity, belongs to Barbara Byers: intellectual comrade, willing reader, irreverent critic, and beloved life companion of almost a quarter century now. To all of you, thank you.

FIRST LAUGH

THE AMERICAN PEOPLE

The congressman stands on the Senate steps. He adjusts this season's fashionable pink tie and the little electronic receiver continually threatening to slip from his ear, and faces the camera head-on. Which has him facing us. The reporter makes short shrift of the usual pleasantries: "Thank you, Congressman, for being willing to talk to us tonight." The congressman smiles and says it's his pleasure. I know what's coming next. Whatever the issue, whatever the question about it, and regardless of whether the spokesperson is a Democrat, a Republican, or an Independent, within the next thirty seconds he or she will use the catch-all phrase, "The American People." I can bet my future on it.

This is supposed to mean me.

The term "American People" is presumed to be one with which I can identify. I was born here, I'm a citizen,[1] and although I prefer "U.S. American" to "American"—Mexicans, Canadians, Bolivians, and Chileans, indeed all the peoples of these continents claimed by Amerigo Vespucci, claim equal right to the name American—when I hear the reference these days I have trouble subscribing. And I do hear the reference all the time: at least thirty and counting in last night's newscast alone.

"The American People want . . . feel . . . need . . . are upset with . . . won't stand for . . ." One can finish these pronouncements in any number of ways but the claim still runs roughshod over our sensibilities. "It's the American People's money." That's even more ludicrous. I can't remember anyone asking me if I wanted my tax dollars to go to the war in Iraq, used to bail out a crooked bank, or line the pockets of those who participated in one of the many pyramid schemes currently robbing this country's workers of their homes, jobs, pension plans, and health care. When I am told that we, the American People, now own 80 percent of AIG, the insurance giant deemed "too large to fail," I would find it funny if it weren't so infuriating. Sure, my dollars and those of millions of others are being used for these bailouts, but no one asked if I agree with the forced investment.

No one ever asked me what I think of the company's devious schemes, "creative" accounting, ongoing theft, layoffs of thousands, and hefty rewards to a few. In the case of AIG I have even heard the idea—could it really be intended as reassuring?—that since the American People now own 80 percent of the company, we should be able to get it to rectify its ways. Perhaps this is some new sort of joke. The more than half-million citizens losing their jobs each month aren't laughing.

Neither am I.

"The American People believe" and "the American People trust" are just as outrageous. To begin with, there are profound differences in background, situation, and expectations among the almost three billion who call ourselves Americans. The Idaho potato farmer (white, male, immigration safely obscured in a distant past, and inheritor of the struggling family farm), inner-city teenager (Hispanic, third-generation gang member, suspended from middle school for the sixth time this year), Native American poet (female, inventor of a new language that draws by turns on hip-hop and her people's long tradition, whose intimate need is to get her family to acknowledge and support her sexuality), and African American pastor (who just happens to be Presbyterian) are as different as if they were from different countries.

The sixteen-year-old computer geek already working on communication for the next generation, the recently middle-class but newly homeless family huddled inside one of the makeshift shelters in Sacramento's growing tent city, the great-grandmother training for a super-marathon, the young man who enlisted for war when there were no jobs to be had, and the daughter of undocumented workers who was born here but walks the painful bridge between family and community every single day. All are U.S. Americans. And all live lives as different from one another as may be possible to imagine. Their physical landscape is varied. In some cases they would seem to inhabit different centuries. Not even the languages they speak, and certainly not their dreams, can be assumed to be the same.

Plenty of us are angry and ever so articulate at voicing that anger, but those with their fingers on the buttons and pens poised above the blank checks don't seem to be listening. It's condescending at best and insulting at worst to be reminded that our government and corporations are acting in our best interests, on our behalf, or in our name, when none of the decision making accrues to us. We get to vote for those whose stated opinions most closely resemble our own, but there is always a distance between the campaign promise and the intention or ability to fulfill that promise once in office.

Polls commonly provide the statistics backing claims that 13 or 51 or 67 percent of the American People favor this or that. Who gets polled? Usually a sample of two or three hundred, often less. Those taking the calls, who don't mind being interrupted in the middle of dinner, don't work the night shift, don't live at a homeless shelter, and aren't troubled by yes or no responses around issues so clearly requiring caveat and contextualization. More important, who sponsors and funds these polls? Quite often a lobbying firm or news outlet that predictably targets the population and encourages the answers that most convincingly support its interests.

The American People per se is a meaningless and insulting label: populist and bombastic. It's as absurd a promise as "lose forty-two pounds in three weeks" or "ten easy lessons guaranteed to teach you conversational Chinese," and every bit as misleading. Beneath the easy rhetoric a double-edged sword lies in wait, dangerous to us as individuals and as a community of neighbors.

One edge of the blade is false patriotism, the simplistic assumption that posits My Country Right or Wrong. We all want to be proud of our country and what it stands for, but few of us pause to consider where extreme nationalism can lead. The other edge preys on our healthy need to belong—to a family, group, or nation. It is a need that has come down through prehistory and history, and it speaks to our very instinct for survival. But it can as easily translate into religious fanaticism or gang membership as into community spirit.

I'm a poet, a writer, and language is my primary currency. Perhaps for this reason I so deeply value precision of speech, want to learn to say exactly what I mean at all times. If we do not begin to call things by their names, we will never know what they are, what they really mean, and how they affect us. Before the second wave of feminism, when we used to say "I was assaulted" or "I was raped" rather than "such and such a person assaulted me" or "so and so raped me," the unnamed passive tense protected the perpetrator and made accountability impossible. If we cannot demand that we ourselves be named correctly, we will be forced to accept every lie that threatens to complete the design of our own annihilation.

I am a U.S. American woman because I was born in this country, although I've lived significant years of my life in several others and carry their landscapes on my skin. Independent of those years away, I am fed by other races and ethnicities, genders and identities, just as I am fed by the rushing river and long shadows of a canyon called Grand. I am a mother and grandmother.

Our national census classifies me as Caucasian. I descend from European Jews but am secular and Socratic in my beliefs. I have loved men, and for the past quarter century have loved a woman who is my life companion. Our relationship is unrecognized by my country's laws, which does nothing to diminish its depth and beauty but deprives us both of rights enjoyed by heterosexual citizens. I am a feminist, not because I am a lesbian but because I am human. I am an artist and social activist— meaning I have not given up on participating with the few to build a world of justice for the many. And at this writing I am seventy-four years old, a time of life that enables me to look back as well as forward, and weigh my particular mix of experience and knowledge in ways still unavailable to the young.

I don't think "American People" begins to cover the strength and subtleties of my identity, not even a little. And not even my country's pollsters, corporate media, manufacturing industry, or advertising experts really think so either. Their awareness of difference can be plainly seen in the sophisticated ways in which they categorize and target each and every one of us according to class, race, gender, age, income, and other consumer-oriented variables.

So when I hear "American People," I don't feel alluded to.

And this is not simply a matter of semantics or misplaced labels. With this skewed use of language comes another and much more dangerous spin-off: we ourselves are encouraged to gloss over our differences; we begin to think of ourselves as The American People—en masse. This only reinforces the old melting pot myth. We belong to what would seem to be a privileged club. While striving for the Dream, we assimilate to the lowest common denominator, and this keeps us from understanding real diversity in all its richness, pathos, and possibility.

Another frequent plea these days is "we must make the American People whole" or—since those with the power to do so are spending so much of our money in ways not of our choosing— "make the taxpayer whole." When billions in taxpayer money was pumped into a major bank about to go under, and it was revealed that after taking the money the company's CEO authorized large sums to be spent on sumptuous island getaways and extravagant bonuses given to those high-level executives whose failed policies had orchestrated the rip-off in the first place, chagrined lawmakers began talking about what might be done to make the taxpayer whole.

Is that me they're talking about?

I pay my taxes on time and in full, but no one asked my opinion. And I'm not naïve enough to offer it—except in some non-electoral venue: by signing a petition or taking part in a public rally. I'm not sure these money games—transparently corrupt and purposefully overcomplicated—can ever make a person whole. How do you make people whole after laying them off and foreclosing on their homes? Only by putting them back to work and giving them another place to live. Anything less really doesn't cut it.

I might approve, but certainly wouldn't inhabit wholeness, if our country's elected officials announced they had found a way to keep that bank's fat cats from getting their obscene bonuses. Why? Because I'd know that even as a couple dozen had to give up their second jet or upcoming trip to some private playground, many thousands of others would be plotting new and more foolproof ways to take advantage of the endless loopholes our system offers the rich.

Wholeness to me is about health and well-being for every man, woman, and child, a lessening of violence and nurturing of compassion, an embrace of health, creativity, culture, art, and humor. My needs are modest. I might feel I was being made whole, at least momentarily, if someone slowed down when he saw I was trying to change highway lanes, and let me into his. If the checkout person at the grocery store realized I'd picked up a more expensive version of an item they had on sale for less, and offered to make the switch. If someone asked me "How ya doing?" and actually waited for a reply, demonstrating that the question was more than mere formality.

I draw these examples from the minutiae of everyday exchange. There are others much more vital to our well-being.

Curing someone of a terminal disease might make that person whole. Healing an aching heart as well. Providing solace and safety to a battered woman, traumatized veteran, abused child, or abandoned human being of any sex or age: these are gifts that may help to initiate a journey to wholeness.

Making it possible for a man born in a woman's body or a woman born in a man's to finally achieve the identity for which they have yearned: this is making whole in ways the rest of us cannot imagine. When being sick entitles us all to the care we need to get well, and no one must travel abroad for a procedure beyond his means at home, I can tell you I will feel gratefully whole.

As the U.S. occupation of Iraq wears on and soldiers are forced to serve two, three, and more tours of duty, their mental health is being frayed as never before. Domestic abuse among returning veterans has increased dramatically. Incidents of suicide among both on-duty personnel and returning veterans have reached epidemic proportions. Soldier-on-soldier murder is also up. At Fort Campbell, Kentucky, in May of 2009, the base was ordered to a three-day stand-down to address the number of suicides at the facility. Yet despite pleas for appropriate attention all the way up and down the military ladder, horribly traumatized soldiers still are not receiving the help they need. They are still not being made whole.[2]

This is due, at least in part, to a cultivated sense of sameness. Members of the U.S. military are supposed to be tough—without exception. Asking for help denotes weakness. And even those who dare to ask are often overlooked or turned away. A John Wayne culture shaped through generations applauds those who get by as they can and punishes those who threaten the façade.

Rarely do we talk about the hundreds of thousands of Iraqis

8

maimed, murdered, displaced, and traumatized by George W. Bush's war. I will feel plenty whole when the last U.S. invader leaves Iraq. But this is because I consider myself to be a member of the human family, and as long as Iraq remains occupied, so am I. When the Palestinians enjoy an unthreatened homeland, I too will experience a sense of wholeness. When troubled children in our own inner-city schools are no longer considered and treated like throwaways, that may do it for me too.

The wholeness I seek is also plural, meaning it's usually not about me alone. It is about what connects me to others, what brings us together and creates those bridges that make life so gratifying: between lovers, friends, parents, and children, generations separated by millennia; and for that matter between dolphins, lions, gazelles, horses, and every other animal. It is the wholeness that comes when the easy fulfillment of need is unburdened by social hypocrisy or grotesque fundamentalist dogma. Wholeness, indeed, may be a feedback loop.

I can be made whole by a sunset so orange and pink and dusky purple it imprints itself upon my eyes, a chance to gaze at the light of day receding from a deep canyon until only its highest rim of rock is tinged in gold, the sound of wind moving through the pale green leaves of a cottonwood tree in spring, a doe sudden and still along a mountain trail, a baby whale leaping like a sleek little pickle from the churning Pacific. Wholeness engulfs me when I stand in the ruins of an ancient civilization, imagining the people who inhabited it and experiencing the connection that prompts me to ask questions already answered in their long-ago lives. These are the questions that guide me now.

PUMPING GAS

Again I am somewhere else. Or everywhere at once. But as always, every word has its color. Sometimes, when I lose one now, the color rises behind my eyes but the word still plays hide-and-seek. Taunts me from the sidelines. Or a vast rainbow looms, and I must find my way through hues and the language they mask. Sometimes I sit for long minutes sifting through color on my way to word. Word may try to resist, but synapse eventually takes me home.

I am seventy-four. My father died of Alzheimer's. He was in his late eighties, but still. In retrospect there'd been years of signs: unmistakable, some even dramatic. Like getting up in the dark of night, demanding breakfast from Mother. Or taking a small list from his pocket to help him order at a restaurant. Several years before he died, he confessed to having forgotten how to subtract. "Can you teach me?" he asked Barbara and me. We couldn't. A man who was characteristically sweet and—despite all predictions to the contrary—became more so in his final months. Still, denial, like a web, trapped every family member. When denial crashed, the before and after mocked us all.

My father's story inhabits mine like a prehistoric animal ready to spring. Thought fragments, a sentence misplaces its tail, and I wonder, wonder. Now every lost word draws an exclamation from someone, surely meant to console but I feel them as condescending: "I know . . . I know what you feel . . . it happens to me, all the time."

I consider contamination from pesticides, hormones, food additives, water, power plants and their billowing stench. I think about how our exposure to radiation from medical screening has grown seven-fold between the early 1980s and 2006.[1] I can see the once-pristine landscape, surrounding the desert majesty of Shiprock, where monster chimneys spew invisible smoke and people keep getting sick. What we breathe, without thinking about it. Toxic waste: corporate gift to so many poor communities.

Now I maneuver the car into the crowded Chevron station, pulling into the space beside the only available pump. Exaggerated satisfaction: I've managed to position myself with the car's tank on the appropriate side. But other storylines continue to intrude. Again I am somewhere else.

There have been so many cars since my first, a muddy-brown Austin more than half a century behind me now. I bought that one for $500 in my early twenties, then sold it for the same amount days before it broke down for good.

I've always named my cars. Mónica, after Mónica Ertl, the Bolivian woman who hid Inti Peredo[2] in her home during Latin

America's cruel era of dirty wars. Hortensia, for the kind Cuban woman who cared for my youngest daughter when political repression in Mexico forced us to send the children on ahead. Much more recently, Biko: after Bantu Steven Biko, tortured to death in an Apartheid prison in 1984.

Just one more way of honoring risk and courage. This last name recycles itself; I continue to use it for a succession of replacement vehicles—always referring to them as she.

Slowing down, smiling in spite of myself, I think about the gray-blue Studebaker coupe my parents let me drive through my last two years of high school. The one I would leave by the side of more than one New Mexico country road when heading out with a Geological Survey map in hand, following the rises and hollows of the land, passionate to believe I could escape Civilization. With a capital C.

Mid last century: the world was safer then and a young girl could explore that world—its colors and meaning—without a shaming fear. I still delight in memories of those nights spent alone, stretched naked on some warm desert rock, imagining myself before the conquerors arrived. Sometimes before the presence of any human.

There were a few Datsuns, including the one we sold for quick cash when escaping Mexico City, 1969. Then, in Cuba, the little badly painted bright blue Datsun sedan whose brakes were always failing and whose floor eventually rusted through. I lost that car in one surprising moment when the government confiscated it, claiming it belonged to my ex-husband who'd left the country months before. Such were the contradictions in a revolution often betrayed by anachronism even as it strove for future.

I think about noise pollution, and the confusion brought by

avalanches of information. Text messaging, cell phoning, all manner of off-stage conversation assaulting the ear. Nowhere can we escape it now, from highway to airport gate area, restaurant to waiting room. Era of the Internet, pushing us further from one another even as it joins us at the hip. True, the elderly aren't the only ones who forget a word, the end of a sentence, why they're holding that particular item in their hands, what they plan to do next. These days ever younger people show symptoms of overload. But on the downhill edge of life it feels unidirectional.

In contrast, perhaps even in direct relationship, age has brought me a new awareness. Unexpected but unmistakable: as memory ruptures along my particular fault lines, difficult to claim. It is as if the last few elusive pieces have fallen into place. I hold the larger picture in slightly trembling hands.

Despite a gnawing discomfort around Volkswagen's relationship with the Third Reich, I, like so many of my generation, drove my share of Beetles. In the mid-1960s my young family and I coaxed one across the Mohave Desert, heat stuck in the on position and all its windows gaping. Since my 1984 return to the United States, there've been two comfortable Jettas. Then a used Volkswagen van that hauled what Barbara and I took cross-country when I got that first year's teaching job at Trinity in 1986.

We couldn't sell that van for half what we'd paid for it. Priding ourselves on being tough when it comes to cars, yet losing, always losing. And one last Volkswagen, a diesel: just as the price of that once-cheap fuel rose above the cost of regular gasoline. Wherever it went that vehicle trailed its parts: a mirror, a hubcap, handle, or knob.

Until we traded it in on our first Toyota. The white Corolla supplemented the also white four-wheel drive Jeep. So dependable, that Jeep: Emma was her name, after Emma Goldman, who said she didn't want a revolution if you couldn't dance in it. It transported us along miles of back roads in search of ancient petroglyphs, ruins unlisted on any map. We still needed two cars back then, and the Corolla had a trunk that could accommodate Mother's walker: a Mafia trunk, we joked, big enough for a body-sized block of cement destined for some deep-water grave.

After moving from the foothills into the city, Barbara and I were determined to go to a single car. We'd been together two decades by then and the decision was one more milepost on this map of shared aging. We sold the Jeep we'd only used a couple of times its last year—each pre-trip discussion pitting the advantage of off-road travel against its poor 16 MPH.

For a while, then, it was just the Corolla: easy sharing, good mileage, and the satisfaction of a reduced footprint in a world panting its way through these waning years of fossil fuel. Believing we could save our earth, one effort at a time.

Until that Saturday when I put a slow roast in the oven and we went food shopping, never expecting we'd detour via the Toyota dealership and—just for kicks—test-drive a Prius. Now the footprint is smaller still, the hybrid our only family car. Barbara, fifteen years younger than me, mostly rides her bike or scooter. She also handles vehicle maintenance, including filling them up.

Which is probably why, I tell myself, I sit beside this pump unable to remember how to open the little door implacably shielding the gas tank.

Everything grows very still. I finger the knobs and dials on steering wheel and dash, try to recall what unlatched that flush little door on Mónica's hip, on Hortensia or Emma. Nothing useful floats to the surface. Stay calm, I tell myself. I remember the manual in its navy plastic envelope and open the glove compartment. "Gas"—in the index—"page 78."

But again I am somewhere else. Page 78 doesn't seem to have any information about accessing the fuel tank. Could Toyota have made a mistake? I read it again, slowing my respiration after every sentence; then the previous page and the one following. Clear instructions for how to open the trunk or roll down windows, but nothing about that little door.

People are honking now. Just behind me a guy in a Humvee stares. I avoid his eyes, go back to the manual, read the text again.

Still nothing.

Take a deep breath, I tell myself. This can't be this hard. Somewhere on page 78 the answer must be hiding. Start again, from the top. Is this about memory, or sight, or something else? I reread and the words come into focus, where they've always been: a small lever on the floor to the left of my seat, right beside the driver's door. I look down. The white gas tank icon on the black tab stares back.

With a grateful hand I reach, tap the lever, release the latch. As I get out of the car I glance to make sure the little door is really open. I insert and then quickly remove my credit card from the pump's slot, remembering earlier times when I'd have saved a few pennies with Self Serve while others handed their key to an attendant who pumped gas, checked oil and tire pressure, and wiped windshields for a tip.

The little screen says my credit card has been approved. Then the message changes: "Remove nozzle. Pump gas." I'm on automatic again as I press the button for regular grade, dislodge the nozzle, and pull the hose to my car's waiting tank. Again, I am somewhere else. Or everywhere at once.

Without denying support for wars of national liberation, I can finally embrace pacifism as the only entirely rational answer. War is always horror. Capital punishment is obscene, no matter the obscenity of the crime. Nationalism itself bears reexamination, as it invariably leads to positions of exception, overarching authority, and swollen ego. Too many authoritarian leaders, too much dynasty. And far too many dead who believed they were dying for something different. Their faces wander in my dreams. Their presence, too, bothers my ability to remember.

Return. Reclaim. *Reclamar*: somewhere between to retrieve and demand.

Tragically, this is how we have raised our men, generation to generation. Not this man or that—your brother or husband, my son—but male people in a system that supports and encourages their basest instincts. A seed born in some deep construct of inferiority sprouts and grows through bullying to war and uncontrolled domination, taking over as the illness of violence.

Religion provides a perfect framework for this distortion; it is the very basis for a division among peoples: those in command and their followers. From popes to gurus, the narcissistic personality claims everything in its path. Class, race, and cultural tradition: all are part of the picture. William James was right when he said the church, in spite of whatever human goodness it may foster, can be counted on as a staunch ally in every attempt to stifle the spontaneous spirit.

I have come to believe that religion also stifles curiosity, knowledge, imagination, and truth: Joan of Arc, Giordano Bruno, Galileo, and Archbishop Oscar Romero.[3] And of course human rights: to life, love, and equal protection under the law. Women, lesbians, and gay men stagger at the bottom of the heap, our rights or lack thereof dependent upon the culture in which we live. Justice is always simpler than the experts would have us think.

The Humvee driver looks belligerent now. He displays no visible relief that I've solved the problem and am pumping the gas.

Today everything's Self Serve. And automatic. No human on the other end of the telephone line, just a recorded voice following the answer to each successive question with a cheerfully upbeat, perfectly inflected "All right then, let's keep going!" as if there really is someone there, paying attention to my need. "Listen carefully, as our menu has changed. Press 1 if . . . press 2 if . . ." Oblivious to my frustration, the fact that mine is not a yes or no question. Multiple choice doesn't cut it.

What passes for progress.

Although we span a considerable age difference, memory and its rough terrain are areas Barbara and I inhabit together. Anguish and understanding: a balance sought. I remember a time a while back when she was visibly frightened that I was stumbling toward the downward spiral; I must have done or failed to do, said or failed to say, something important. I caught worried looks, whispered consultations with others. Tension mounted until she understood her degree of concern might itself damage what we have. Despite the age difference, we both clearly suffer from varieties of forgetting: mine undoubtedly more age-related, hers resulting from extreme childhood abuse.

Collateral damage is so often expressed as afterthought. And not only on the battlefield but also in the world of economic exchange and security: credit and derivatives and bundles and foreclosures and leveraged debt. An intentionally complicated swamp, meant to blur the simple fact of a family evicted from its home, a person ousted from his or her job, health and well-being beyond reach, a future disappearing beneath such a heavy blanket of greed, or a simple task waiting to be undertaken.

Despite the unrelenting—often mixed—messages, overall sleight of hand is painfully transparent. The latest corporate scheme translates to gross theft: of sustenance and identity. As long as we fail to look through any eyes but our own, as long as every androcentric, egocentric viewpoint guides our vision, we doom ourselves to extinction. Human rights. Animal rights. The right of earth itself.

Nowhere is our vision narrower or more skewed than in our eternal search for life in distant parts of the universe, or in other universes. We seem unable to grasp the fact that other worlds are likely to have given birth to life forms adapted to their discrete conditions. Why should they look or act like us?

Which brings me back to my renewed certainty: justice really is quite simple. I remember believing this when I was very young, not yet privy to all the theories and counter-theories. Along the way, major texts and charismatic figures convinced me otherwise. Experience consolidated those convictions. Isms. Schisms within isms. Then, painfully, the unraveling. A hunger for power and insatiable greed dressed differently for every new occasion.

What was sacrificed was always "necessary." Except of course for those forced to make the sacrifices. The ends never justify the means. I reject the image of a no-man's land. Fence-sitting and its devil's advocates. It looks to me like a land of nothingness, where familiarity eats away at invisible contours, false promises of relief. Where identity is spliced and dignity dies.

Oh those colors: still brilliant in my aging eyes. Losing the sharpness of youth. Taking longer to arrange an image in the lens, camera less sure in my shaking hands. No longer able to drive at night, the oncoming headlights exploding my sight. But oh, those colors pulsing within colors! Cream and orange-red, pink and desert-varnish brown, as far as I can see. Waning light running along a lip of rock. The seam where river meets wall. My landscape: prying me open, filling me up.

I get back in my car and sit for a moment. The Humvee driver waits. Before pulling out I turn and look him calmly in the eye. I force myself to hold the gaze, silently counting to ten. Another advantage of age: no apologies.

Of course I wonder how or if to tell Barbara about my difficulty accessing the gas tank. Then I promise myself I will. We are in this together.

FLYING BACKWARD

Not backward as in eyes in the back of their heads. Backward as in turning around, traveling in the opposite direction. Going north instead of south. Scientists and ordinary people have noticed that many birds have been migrating to higher rather than lower latitudes these days, in search of the temperature they need in order to winter successfully. Our human-caused climate change has turned their maps on end. Instinct breaks with tradition in the search for survival.

It seems when it comes to global warming, the canary in the coal mine isn't a canary; it's a purple finch or swallow. All those smaller birds that pack the loudest message. A 2008 Audubon Society study found that more than half of 305 bird species in North America, including robins, gulls, chickadees, and owls, are now wintering about thirty-five miles farther north than they did forty years ago. Over these forty years the average January temperature in the United States climbed by about five degrees Fahrenheit, a dramatic increase and a warning that can only be ignored at our peril.

Global warming does not, of course, simply raise the earth's temperature. It melts the northern and southern ice caps, thus raising the level of oceans and robbing polar bears of their habitat. It makes the earth's surface darker so less light and heat are reflected, and blows dirt across pristine expanses of snow. It reshapes deserts, creates new mating and birthing fields while invalidating others, and changes foraging and grazing patterns. It produces violent storms and causes devastating fires and floods. Temperatures rise in some places while falling in others. And all this seems to happen erratically; new patterns are either just beginning to form or are as yet too large for us to see them clearly.

Birds are not the only creatures to feel the impact; as climates change and growing seasons are affected, famine assaults ever greater numbers of large mammals and human beings. The great whales change course. Life in all its diversity is thrown off balance, perhaps in ways that foreshadow its demise. Still, birds provide us with a powerful warning. I think of Bosque del Apache, the marshes and wetlands so carefully tended as an avian refuge an hour and a half south of Albuquerque. We visit several times a year to view the thousands of sandhill cranes clustered together then rising off the surface of water that pulses with the reflection of a setting sun. The snow geese like plump little circles of white who appear to nest on water's surface.

I can remember a decade ago when we saw the larger whooping cranes there as well, a count of five or six per season. Then there were two, finally one, and for years now there haven't been any. The absence of such creatures leaves a permanent ache. My lungs still breathe in tandem with theirs. If the great number of birds that winter at Bosque del Apache each year were to be forced farther north, I try to imagine where they might end up: on some dry sustenance-lacking desert? In the smog of the metropolis?

The discovery of birds flying north instead of south is mostly based on data collected during the Audubon Society's annual Christmas Bird Count. This is when birders young and old come out in large numbers to count the different species. Sighting a sparrow or hawk and entering it on a list, these passionate amateurs further the science of ornithology and add to our data about migratory patterns, new or abandoned habitats, and overall climate change. The birds tell the people and the people inform the scientists. The weak link—the place where failure to act takes its greatest toll—is between scientists and government. In almost every arena, policy lags far behind the problem it is meant to fix. Will we never catch up? And if we do will it be too late? There are island nations in the Pacific that will disappear beneath the sea in a matter of decades.

The question might better be posed: do we want to catch up? The failure of government to address the issue of climate change can be traced to two sources. On the one hand, short-term greed: corporations and individuals who would rather line their pockets today than worry about what life will be like for their children or grandchildren down the road. Government caters to, when it is not owned by, these corporations. On the other, religious fundamentalism: that variety of arrogant ignorance that provides such a handy justification for refusing to learn. In fundamentalist belief systems God gave man dominion over the earth; whatever he does to it can easily be ascribed to carrying out God's will. Belief in Armageddon also absolves men and their institutions of responsibility. This blind spot or denial is very much at the crux of the problem, and has been surprisingly little discussed.

Confusing seasons, angering wind and rain, forcing wildlife to explore unknown terrain, and killing off whole species are not reckonings we should take lightly. The web of life as it has developed down through millennia has created a complex interdependency in which a bird thrown off course along our Pacific seaboard may thwart the reproduction of frogs in Africa. If the rancher who shoots a Mexican wolf in southeastern New Mexico thinks only of his livestock, his grandchild may die of the sort of hunger he believed only affected the "other": that swollen-bellied vacant-eyed fly-infested child he never learned to see as human.

Today religious fundamentalism of every stripe and in many nations is the greatest obstacle to rational thought and justice, the end to violence and wars, and a healing of the earth. The Bible-thumping Christian who would replace evolution with creationism in our pitifully backward public education, or attack women's reproductive rights—going so far as to murder abortion doctors—while caring nothing for the millions of starving children who already struggle to survive. The Muslim fundamentalist who issues contracts on the lives of those who do not believe as he does, and keeps women covered and controlled. The Jew whose legitimate longing for a safe homeland leads him to uproot and oppress his Palestinian relatives. A military establishment that puts its war games before whales. Industries that would sacrifice our remaining wild places to the profits they can make in oil. A cultural memory so short it would trade an increased production of genetically modified corn for the ancient message of natural seed regeneration.

Some may say I am confusing religious zeal with millennial belief systems, military requirements, or corporate growth. I say they are already linked. Power lures, and blind faith justifies all manner of abuse. We have only to remember how Christian fundamentalists declared George W. Bush's presidency "the will of God," or how Bush himself justified outrageous policy decisions because God assured him they were right. Alternately, we have Islam's fundamentalist suicide bombers who blow up innocents—among them so many children—in the name of their twisted cause. And across all latitudes and cultural divides, the routine abuse of women and children so often justified by some so-called sacred text.

An example of such religious zeal here in the United States was the attempt on the part of some in Dover, Pennsylvania, a few years back, who wanted to mandate the teaching of something called intelligent design along with evolution in that town's middle schools. Several fundamentalist Christians got themselves elected to the local school board. They presented the change as a matter of fairness: if evolution is a theory, they argued, why not teach another theory as well? Instead of the scientifically discredited creationism, they coined the term *intelligent design*, which they hoped might prove more palatable. When interviewed by a reporter, one of its proponents simply quoted the Bible: "'And God created heaven and earth.' That's enough for me," he added, a self-righteous conviction blazing in his eyes.

Science teachers and parents fought back, and in 2005 Dover was the site of a much-publicized trial. After months of expert testimony presented by both sides, and in spite of the fact that the judge himself was a devout Christian the evolutionists feared might not be able to hear their arguments, the proponents of intelligent design were defeated. All those members of the Dover school board who had taken the fundamentalist position were also voted out of office. In this case reason triumphed. In many others it hasn't.

But it wasn't this win alone that held my attention. I was intrigued by one of the scientist's testimony, in which he explained the difference between theory and fact. The creationists insisted that since evolution is "only a theory, not a fact," other theories should be presented as well. The theory was presumed to be tentative and thus subject to easy attack, while facts were unassailable. But this scientist explained that facts also change as new information is discovered, while theories are tested and accepted until another theory comes along that is capable of refuting its "truth." Process as opposed to product.

I realized that I myself had sometimes confused theory with fact and went to the dictionary for a definition of each:

"Theory. A coherent group of general propositions used as principles of explanation for a class of phenomena."

"Fact. The quality of existing or of being real; actuality; truth." And further down on the list: "Something said to be true or supposed to have happened." In other words, assumed to be true until scientific testing or later discovery proves otherwise.

It all reduces to the dogma of closed minds. A failure to ask questions rather than the humility implicit in listening to their answers and the wisdom to build upon those answers.

Walking through Athens's public forum half a millennium before the advent of our era, Socrates may or may not have been able to imagine how his particular way of reproducing knowledge would unfold through the centuries: the questions he asked and how, the insights that led to further questions, what we now call the Socratic method. We only know the man, after all, through Plato's writings. Walking among the ruins of that same forum a few years back, I felt a current coursing through my body. My skin came alive, charged by recognition. I thought my hair must be standing out in wild configuration. Every bone in my body moved me forward: open, excited, ready.

It was as if I were walking the narrowest of bridges from discovery to discovery, truth to truth, stepping into a physical space that would later—simultaneously before, during, and after my own existence—witness the births of all those other great minds, each having to battle the dogma and fear of his or her day to further our knowledge of who and where we are. Socrates. Galileo. Giordano Bruno. Spinoza. Darwin. Rachel Carson. Laurette Sejourne. Adrienne Rich. Ruth Hubbard. (There is a reason the names of the men on this very partial list are household words while the women's are much less so. Fundamentalism also plays a part in maintaining gender inequality, so useful in silencing more than half the human race.)

Independent of their gender, all those great minds were shut down or, in more forgiving times, evicted from the canon, thrown out of the academy, ignored by conservative societies. All were considered heretics by the fundamentalism of their time and place. Even in the twenty-first century, the entire small town of Dover, Pennsylvania, took a risk when it challenged an attempt by Christian fundamentalists to pass creationism off as science in its schools. We owe a permanent debt of gratitude to all those brave men and women. They stand out among the many we have to thank that life has not yet been extinguished. Not yet.

The more tolerant among us, those who come down on the side of live and let live, don't always think about the real harm the fundamentalist mind-set does to our political analyses, educational and legal systems, intellectual exploration, artistic and scientific creativity, human rights record, and social interaction overall. We will never know how many beautiful minds and spirits are prevented from blossoming into the sort of genius that imbues our lives with richness and pushes us forward to new levels of discovery. Like racism and sexism, fundamentalist limitations on knowledge greatly diminish our nation's ability to draw on its best talents.

Our pundits and even many elected officials are fond of pointing out that education in the United States is "the best in the world." It isn't, and it continually astonishes me that this affirmation is so rarely challenged. From elementary school to postgraduate studies, we lag far behind European, Asian, African, and many Latin American institutions. Basic education has been burdened almost beyond repair by wrong-headed and inefficient mandates such as No Child Left Behind.

U.S. public education has been dealt a serious setback by an exaggerated emphasis on testing. Students are no longer encouraged to engage in complex thought processes. Because it is tied to school funding, scoring well is the goal; and rigging tests or fudging results is more common than many know.

Scientific work was dealt a blow by the George W. Bush administration when it refused to fund embryonic stem cell and other important medical research. This put our scientists at a disadvantage when compared with those in the other industrially advanced countries. Obama has reversed this policy, but continuity has been lost.

Human rights in the United States, so diminished since 9/11 but still so loudly proclaimed as among the most complete internationally, have been eroded by fundamentalist values on a variety of fronts, among them the continued existence of capital punishment in many states, limitations on women's reproductive rights, the right of homosexuals to enjoy the legal benefits of their heterosexual counterparts, and the right of the terminally ill to die with dignity.

At one of the bookstores at Grand Canyon a couple of years back, I picked up a book that claims the canyon was formed by Noah's flood four thousand years ago. If it were not so pathetic it might be a joke. Here we have the National Park Service, a government dependency supported by taxpayer money, promoting a fundamentalist view of prehistory. I can only hope the Obama administration will rectify such embarrassing manifestations.

Toward the end of our last presidential campaign, when Barack Obama uttered one brilliantly coherent speech after another and John McCain felt pressured to launch a last oppositional volley, we saw how fundamentalism makes a weapon of ignorance; at least one of its techniques was painfully clear. This was when the Republicans produced Sarah Palin, a proudly unlettered cheerleader type who proclaimed the "real" America to be those places where drinking beer and waving flags take center stage.

But if we look a bit deeper at the dichotomy established, we can see it wasn't simply about low brow versus high brow. We can discern much deeper and more complex references to fundamentalist ideas about asking questions, valuing or ridiculing knowledge, intellect versus faith. Suddenly "eloquent" became a dirty word, as suspect as "liberal" several campaign cycles earlier. When Obama made a particularly good speech, his opponent accused him of eloquence. A brilliant mind was even placed in opposition to experience, as if both could not reside within the same person.

It didn't take long for me to realize that eloquence in this context was code for the devil. Among Christian fundamentalists those who dare to question are told the devil is speaking through them, trying to possess their souls. They must resist the devil's temptation. The very act of questioning is equated with evil. Knowledge is sin, ignorance becomes a virtue, and salvation can be achieved only through blind faith. In a country in which the influence of fundamentalist belief grows exponentially, and where eight years of fundamentalist government have succeeded in diluting separation of church and State and imbuing foreign and domestic policy, the law, education, and everyday discourse with its ugly prejudices, it is possible for a major TV anchor to ask Sarah Palin what news sources she reads and Palin to get away with responding, "I'll get back to you on that."

This is all about an inquiring mind as opposed to one that has been stifled by religious zealotry. It is about encouraging process as opposed to bowing before a flagrant abuse of power that hides behind the claim that blind faith and superstitious belief must rule our lives. It is about waking up, assessing the real danger fundamentalism poses to our lives, and returning to freedom of thought, wherein those who subscribe to its dogma may continue to do so without imposing it on others.

Perhaps one day our birds will no longer be inclined to fly backward.

BIGGER, BETTER, BEST

It is February 25, 2009. We are sitting before the television screen watching our new president, Barack Obama, slowly make his way through the assembly of cheering, hand-shaking, visibly enthusiastic government officials and guests. He has been in office slightly more than a month. Tonight, in the midst of a plunging economy—some call it post-capitalism, others only know they have lost everything—he will speak to both chambers of Congress, members of the Supreme Court, the Pentagon generals in their full-uniform regalia, and, most important, the American people and the world. We already know what his message will be: grave but upbeat, semi-realistic about an economic depression acknowledged in all but name, confident that as citizens of "this great country" we will find a way out. Still, like so many others here and around the world, we will analyze every word, every turn of phrase this young president utters.

I want to talk about one claim in particular, an affirmation repeated daily and by so many here in the United States. It is "this great country," the idea that our country is the richest and most powerful, with the loftiest ideals, a jewel among nations, endowed to take charge by some invisible force—many would say God. The rhetoric urges us to lead by example, while history demonstrates we have most often led by force.

And by continually putting forth the notion that we are the biggest and best, the most powerful, intelligent, inventive—in short, that we possess the ultimate truth: that our way is The Way. As insulting and degrading as this is to others, it also distorts our own sense of self. One of the things Obama said in this speech—he was talking about rebuilding the economy and making it more energy-efficient—was this: "We invented solar technology, but we've fallen behind countries like Germany and Japan in producing it." The second part of this statement is true, but the first leaves a lot to be desired. Solar energy, like so much emerging science, is the product of a number of inventive minds from a number of countries—possible when they resist the temptation to let their gluttony for individual grants and awards keep them from working together. In 1918 a Pole named Czochralski discovered a way to grow single-crystal silicon. Five years later Albert Einstein—a German living in the United States—was awarded the Nobel Prize for his work on solar energy. Scientists of other nationalities continue to refine the process.

Less than a minute later our president went on to say, "We are committed to the goal of a re-tooled, re-imagined auto industry that can compete and win. . . . The nation that invented the

32

automobile cannot walk away from it." Inspiring and energizing as rhetoric, but also at odds with history. The automobile was actually invented in Germany. Gottlieb Daimler, Wilhelm Maybach, and Karl Benz introduced their initial models in 1889. It is true that Henry Ford, here in the United States, achieved first mass production. But this was almost two decades later. The Model T went on sale in 1908.

It may seem that I am taking out of context a couple of small details in an otherwise powerful speech. Along with many, I was moved by the speech. But I believe these erroneous claims to be indicative of something larger and deeply troubling.

And I take issue with another aspect of this bigger and best mentality: the definition of leadership itself. Too often we take for granted that the biggest and best is entitled to lead; certainly that person or corporation or country itself believes this to be true. In this unchallenged assumption leading is transformed into leadership, and the latter is understood as a quality that has earned the right to define the game plan, set a standard, or make the rules. A casual look at power too often assumes it bestows the right to lead.

I believe true leadership must be something else. A genuine leader is someone capable of encouraging and listening to diverse opinions, searching out the best in each, facilitating consensus, and promoting productive change. This is no less true among nations than it is among individuals, and it can only emerge within boundaries of absolute respect.

I came to political consciousness in a bipolar world: the United States on one side, the Soviet Union on the other. Ronald Reagan, our president at the time, dubbed the latter the Evil Empire, setting a tone that encouraged an attitude of disparagement from institutions to individuals. For many years a Cold War culture imbued everything we thought and did with a host of self-righteous claims: our country represented freedom, progress, that to which people everywhere aspired. The Socialist world was portrayed as drab, repressive, one which trampled people's freedoms and destroyed hope. Neither picture was accurate.

But one of these pictures promoted the idea that America was the magical kingdom. U.S. American ingenuity and work ethic are real, and the country did offer opportunities that didn't exist elsewhere. As a consequence our shores were inundated with refugees, documented and undocumented, wanting only a chance at the better life for which we were famous. In fact, everyone seemed to want the American Way of Life. Our educational system, Hollywood films, and a corporate press all reinforced the idea that we were the best and most fortunate.

No wonder everyone wanted a piece of what we had. And how lucky we ourselves were to have been born in this land of limitless possibility! When U.S. tourists travel abroad and their lack of language knowledge makes it hard for them to communicate, they just speak English louder. We are conditioned to think of ourselves as "the one" and everyone else as "other."

I will never forget October 4, 1957, when the Soviet Union put the first artificial satellite into orbit. And not only because it was a news item that gripped the world. Soviet ingenuity affected my own life in ways I would only understand many years later. Sputnik caught the United States by surprise and made our educators realize how deficient our country's math and science education was. As a result, from that moment on those two subjects were given much more attention in the schools.

Because I was a girl I had not been encouraged to understand or even take classes in intermediate mathematics and the sciences. Although education is still profoundly gendered, my generation seemed to be the last in which that sort of sexism stood in the way of a more complete education for girls. After Sputnik those younger than I—girls as well as boys—enjoyed new science and math curricula. After all, we had to compete. And win.

In particular areas this renewed competition paid off. A little more than a decade later, on July 20, 1969, Neil Armstrong—a U.S. American—was the first human being to set foot on the moon. Our space program, too, had been revitalized as a result of Sputnik. When Armstrong radioed back to earth, "That's one small step for man, one giant step for mankind," his words were meant to sound magnanimous and all-inclusive. It was lost on no one, though, that it had been the United States of America that had achieved this epic feat. The astronauts planted a U.S. flag. The amount of money spent since by our space program could surely have lifted the world's neediest out of poverty, stamped out hunger, and perhaps even brought about cures to some of humanity's most insidious illnesses. In a constant state of competition, priorities become terribly skewed.

My son, who studied electrical engineering in Cuba, tells some great stories about the Cold War's parallel mythologies. Each side claimed credit for major discoveries and inventions. One example is the radio. The West said Marconi was its inventor; the Soviets claimed it was Popov—who is reported to have explained wave transmission to the czars, who ignored it. They insisted that Marconi was then able to secure a patent and commercialize the invention. Gregory says one of his professors was lecturing one day, "When Popov invented the radio . . . ," and a student in the back of the lecture hall piped up, "he tuned in the BBC of London." The class erupted in laughter. The students could see the humor, but they were no more able than those of us on this side of the divide to identify the ways in which the era's insane competition influenced their general understanding of world affairs. Like this one there were dozens of other examples. Each claim reinforced a sense of superiority, keeping any real sense of nuance or complexity at bay.

This sense of superiority is blatant in U.S. Americans, and not only when we travel abroad but inside the country as well. It keeps the wealthy scornful of the disadvantaged, men comfortable in their disrespect for women, lighter-skinned people believing they deserve a better deal than people of color, heterosexuals trained not to question the rights they enjoy but to deny their gay sisters and brothers, and so on through a long list of inequalities. Fear of difference defines our relationships, while "My Country Right or Wrong" is the national mind-set substituting belligerence for thought.

Today's economic crisis may be softening the edges of this arrogance just a bit. As more and more people lose their jobs and homes, health care, and pensions, tent cities spring up in many of our major cities. Their inhabitants are no longer the homeless of only a few years back: addicts, the mentally ill, or those pushed out of the system for economic "efficiency." These people were recently middle-class. It is no longer so easy for them to "other" those less fortunate. Still, the sense of bigger, better, best doesn't seem to have changed that much.

The United States was founded on principles of independence from the rule of kings, freedom of religion, respect for philosophical difference, and equality for all peoples; although the pilgrims who invaded these lands built their social structures on the decimation of the original Indian population, African slaves would soon be brought over and forced to build a plantation economy, and neither women nor people of color qualified as full citizens for years. As with every occupation of another's land, gain soon distorted philosophy. Invariably, the ends were tainted by the means.

Despite origins that proposed to prioritize freedom from tyranny, the very fabric of our history is shot through with examples of colonialist plunder and imperialist overreach. The United States has invaded, occupied, and possessed—sometimes simply because it could (and geopolitical advantage or raw materials beckoned), sometimes under the guise of saving the world from one supposed evil or another, and often—as in the recent case of Iraq, justified by flagrant and transparent lies. The era of the Monroe Doctrine wasn't the first nor would it be the last time a U.S. president sought to justify brute expansionism. Theodore Roosevelt is remembered for saying the Nicaraguan dictator Anastasio Somoza was "a son of a bitch, but he's our son of a bitch."

A constitution so brilliant and far-reaching that it has been copied in many parts of the world set our nation apart. Not everyone knows it was modeled on the one written by the Iroquois Confederation of Nations. Its authors did such a good job of seeing into the future that it remains a point of reference for ongoing struggles to improve the rights of all. The sort of semi-representational government established here and fine-tuned over almost three centuries, despite so many failures to live up to its promise, is considered exemplary by many. And a succession of U.S. administrations continues to try to impose it on peoples everywhere. We call it democracy and claim there is nothing better.

Yet with the global crisis something important has changed. The United States of America is no longer the richest country in the world. Today China alone holds enough of our national debt that, were they to call it in, our economic system would collapse. We are no longer the best educated; dozens of other countries do a better job of teaching their young people. Neither are we the healthiest; health care in a number of other countries is more comprehensive, more accessible, and costs less or nothing at all. And those beautiful freedoms? They still exist to a degree unknown in many parts of the world, but eight years of the George W. Bush administration eroded or destroyed them for many. The democracy we have developed has a great many attributes, but so do other systems of government developed by other countries in line with their own histories and cultures.

The facts have changed. How long will it take for the attitudes to catch up? Or, given our propensity for superiority, will they catch up?

Believing we are bigger, better, best may be comforting in the short term but in the long term benefits no one. First of all, because it isn't true, and constantly repackaging the fiction only continues to make us hated throughout the world. No people are superior to others, and believing they are is as morally damaging to those conditioned to think of themselves in that way as it is to those they denigrate or abuse. Secondly, because the assumption of superiority makes true exchange and interaction impossible. Only in conditions of equality can people speak to one another, listen, and learn from each other's experience.

Generation after generation in our country is taught delusions of grandeur and all the moral impoverishment that comes with it.

Eight years of an administration that flaunted this idea in word and action have cost us enormously. When our nation suffered the horrendous terrorist assault of September 11, 2001, a great opportunity presented itself in the midst of extraordinary

38

loss. We might have turned tragedy into a teaching moment, a great national debate about why we had been attacked and how to avoid such pain in the future. This could have been a time when compassion and an understanding of the worthiness of all peoples might have pushed the United States in an entirely different direction. Bush and his cronies were incapable of leading us in that direction; nor did they want to. Their response emanated from the bully position and over time made things much worse. Despite repeated claims that they kept America safe, dangerous stereotypes were reinforced, international terrorism has increased, many hundreds of thousands of lives have been taken, and the world's economy is in shambles. Bigger, better, best may have momentarily seemed like the answer, but did nothing to put us in a more productive or secure relationship with reality.

A second opportunity presented itself with Barack Obama's election. One of his campaign promises was that he would restore world respect for the United States, repair the damage done by his predecessor. In his speeches he has often spoken of coming to listen rather than demand. But a change of image will require more than words. As long as the United States continues to occupy Iraq and Afghanistan, urging other countries to join it in its misadventures, the rest of the world will rightly understand it is being coerced into defending interests it does not share.

The United States is used to being the bully on the playground, seeking through force what it does not have the wisdom to achieve through respect. As long as it really was the strongest power on earth, this attitude—although morally wrong—went relatively unchallenged. Fear is a powerful motivator. Now that we are no longer the richest, strongest, or most powerful, will we be forced to take others into account? We can only hope that wise leadership will emerge.

Barack Obama's ascension to the presidency came with a promise of respect for other peoples, changes in domestic and foreign policy, pledges of transparency, and an end to "business as usual." Perhaps he is sincere and will do something to effect positive change. Yet even in his masterful speeches, we continue to hear about the United States leading, not contributing along with other nations and moving in tandem with them. Patriotism doesn't mean "My Country Right or Wrong." It means applauding my country when right, criticizing it when wrong, and loving it enough to want it to be the best it can be.

I watched Barack Obama's inauguration on CNN in Spanish while visiting two of my children and their families who live in Uruguay. Being outside the country casts our president's message in a broader light than if we listen to it only within the national context. When he spoke about the United States as indisputable world leader, those watching with me exchanged expressions that ranged from tired resignation to indignation. Promising to be less of a bully isn't the same as acknowledging that we are one of many in a broad and diverse world. Our elected officials must begin to recognize this in deed as well as word.

I wonder if I will live long enough to experience an authentic change of heart in this respect, if during my lifetime—or even during my children's or grandchildren's—our nation will be able to engage in a dialogue among equals. Among ourselves and with the world. I long for a day when gratuitous grandstanding is replaced with conversation, when bigger, better, best gives way to wisdom and humility.

RACE AND RACISM

THE 2008 ELECTION

In battering single-mindedness it almost rivaled the O. J. Simpson case of more than a decade before, when all news reports centered on a single item and finding out about anything else going on in the world took some doing. Except now the news was about the first black presidential candidate in U.S. history rather than a black murderer almost everyone knew was guilty, who escaped punishment (at the time) through the expert manipulations of a clever and highly paid black lawyer.

This recent news was much more important to the fabric of our lives, and much more welcome. Indeed, we hung on every word, although much of it was hashed and rehashed to the exclusion of all else. After a year and a half of public discussion about race—most of it superficial, some of it profound, much of it racist—the first black presidential candidate became the first black president-elect, and finally—in drawn-out expectation—the first black president of the United States.

One of the critical moments of the presidential campaign came when Obama's pastor was recorded making what many took as anti-American statements. The corporate press played the episode for all it was worth, and the right-wing media screamed "race!" in a well-calculated attempt at guilt by association. Instead of ignoring the accusation, or fighting back with equally dubious rhetoric, Obama took the opportunity to make a profound and brilliant speech on race.[1] He made it clear that liberals would not be able to purchase racial reconciliation on the cheap. People of almost all persuasions were moved.

After Obama's win, on February 18, 2009, Eric Holder—Obama's attorney general and also an African American—celebrated his first Black History Month in office by speaking to a gathering of Justice Department staff. Among other things, he said "we are a nation of cowards for not talking more about race."[2] The corporate press immediately attacked the comment as unnecessary. Few statements seem more necessary to me.

Race has long quickened the pulse of this country. Racism has been a corrosive burden, especially for those who have suffered from it: the black man accused of looking at a white woman, the black child who couldn't drink from the water fountain, the black woman who couldn't sit at the front of the bus, the vastly disproportionate number of black people imprisoned even today, and black children still routinely receiving inferior public education. We still revere our black sports stars and entertainers while making life as hard as possible for ordinary black youth.

Slavery has shaped our society. Racism also shapes and diminishes those who are educated in its evils and taught to perpetuate its ugly wrongs. The United States can be proud of its powerful Civil Rights Movement, and those who remember its struggles were among the most visibly moved on the night of November 4, 2008. In just forty-five years we had gone from witnessing four little black girls murdered at a Sunday school in Birmingham, Alabama, with no one being brought to trial for the crime, to the election of a black president.[3] These years seem painfully long or astonishingly short, depending on where one is positioned. To many of us they may seem both.

Many have struggled for more equitable race relations, and such relations have improved. But true to the way so much is handled in our society, real in-depth anti-racism work has been slow. During my seventy-four years, we have left behind those trees from which black bodies so often swung in the Deep South, while only a couple of years ago nooses ominously appeared on a tree at a Louisiana college campus and many had the audacity to argue it was simply a boyish prank. Not too many years before that, a black man in Texas was dragged to his death behind a truck driven by racist whites. In my childhood the Ku Klux Klan did its murderous deeds out in the open and with impunity, while in more recent times Klan criminals have been brought to trial, a few even convicted. Black men and women now serve in many high offices (although in minute percentages compared to whites), yet the very same election that brought Barack Obama to the presidency tried to outlaw affirmative action in several states and succeeded in doing so in Michigan.

One of the most talked about phenomena during the 2008 presidential campaign was the Bradley effect, through which it was predicted that many who said they would vote for a black man wouldn't: alone in the voting booth, they just wouldn't be able to do so.[4] If anything, the election results show there was no Bradley effect. Or if there was, it may have operated in reverse. People of color and whites voted for Obama in staggering numbers. Despite a variety of spins on the election results, Barack Obama received landslide approval and a real mandate for change. Some of this vote undoubtedly reflected the disgust and exhaustion voters felt after the George W. Bush years. But much of it reflected their feelings about Obama.

At the same time, Muslims reported feeling happy about the electoral results but marginalized from the debate. Many young Muslims said they hesitated to wear an Obama button for fear they would identify the candidate with a religion and culture so unfairly misunderstood here. More than once during the campaign, when Obama was accused of being a Muslim he responded that he was Christian . . . without asking what would be wrong with his being a Muslim if that were the case. Some Muslim citizens wondered whether to vote their consciences or the stereotype. On the steep ladder of racism there is always one more, lower, rung: always one more category of people to fear and thus hate. The anti-gay initiatives, which carried in several states this election cycle, point to one such category of human beings targeted by those whose "family values" are rooted in hate.

How did a black man ascend to the presidency in a country where racism lives just below the surface of almost every interaction? Perhaps a simple but powerful truth lies outside race. Clearly this was the moment for a candidate who could convince the U.S. public he or she would take the country in a new direction. We—and the entire world—were so tired of George W. Bush, his criminality and lies. People were hurting economically, and violence and mean-spiritedness were being exalted while real human decency was denied. And people were tired of two malignant and seemingly endless wars. If we could choose a candidate who was brilliant, articulate, raised heretofore unheard-of sums of money and mounted a perfect ground organization, we would. And if his opponent—war hero or not—showed himself to be unknowledgeable, opportunistic, erratic, and with poor enough judgment to choose Sarah Palin as his running mate, all the better. Barack Obama was a different kind of candidate, a different kind of person. We—the vast majority of us—elected him. We hoped he would be a different kind of leader.

I have thought a lot about race during and since that long campaign. During the primaries, when I didn't yet know if I favored Hillary Clinton or Barack Obama, I thought about gender and race. I really didn't believe this country was ready to break either of those barriers, and feared the Republicans could win. When Obama achieved the candidacy, I still wondered if a black man could be president. I myself subscribed to the Bradley effect theory. And I don't even think of Obama as a black man, but rather as a man of mixed race (his mother a white woman from Kansas, his father a black man from Kenya, raised by his white maternal grandparents). In other words I think of Obama as truly representative of this multiracial and multicultural country, where in the very near future people of color will outnumber those categorized as white.[5] But in the United States to have even a small amount of black heritage makes one black. In that sense I wondered if it would be possible for people here to elect a "black" president.

Racially speaking, I wonder how Obama thinks of himself. During the long campaign, he had to be so careful when speaking about anything that could be taken out of context and distorted by a mud-slinging opposition. When race threatened to become an issue, he gave a speech that will surely be remembered as one of the high points of thought and feeling in recent political discourse. When asked directly he explained that in America someone like him is black; that's just the way it is. In general he managed to speak more honestly and go deeper about this issue than any candidate in memory. At the same time I suspect Obama describes himself as black for some of the same reasons I describe myself as lesbian. I acknowledge and have lived at various points along the broad curve of sexual identity, but choose to claim the niche that simplifies the issue and also allows me to stand with the most disenfranchised.

And so we did elect a black president. We did it largely because of the youth vote, which Obama supporters got out in record numbers. But whites, Indians, and Latinos also voted overwhelmingly for Obama, and three southern states went for him as well: Virginia, North Carolina, and Florida. The latter was particularly interesting because of its powerful Cuban voting bloc, traditionally conservative and Republican. There generation played an important role. Jorge Mas Canosa, the longtime leader of anti-Castro Cubans, had been dead for a while. Interestingly, both his widow and son endorsed Obama.

Pennsylvania, Ohio, Indiana, Nevada, and New Mexico are other states that weren't expected to go for Obama but did; his ground organization in them was disciplined and spectacular. A variety of post-election polls showed that 43 percent of white, more than 95 percent of black, 67 percent of Latinos, and majority percentages of Asians and Native Americans opted for progressive change. Even among Jews, who had to buck an onslaught of fabricated fear around Obama's supposed abandonment of Israel, 78 percent turned out for him.

There's another group that bears special mention: women.

This time around, 53 percent of voters were women, while only 47 percent of men turned out. Among those voting for Obama, 56 percent were women (despite the Republicans' insulting effort to make us believe we had an advocate in Palin).

These figures were achieved first of all because Obama addressed real issues with thoughtful analysis. And secondly because the Obama organization on the ground worked so hard to increase voter registration and participation at the polls; in other words, it enfranchised millions of Americans by making them believe their opinions can count.

Among African Americans the 11 percent who voted in 2004 rose to 13 percent in 2008. For Latinos the increase was from 8 to 9 percent. For the Indian vote I have only found statistics by tribe; most of these favored the Democrats by very wide margins. But the startling gain, approached warily by many pundits right up to election time, was among the nation's youth. Twenty-four million voters between the ages of eighteen and twenty-four went to the polls, many for the first time. Among them two out of every three chose Obama.

My fear, now, is for those young people. If the Obama administration lets them down, they may well shun electoral politics for life. A man who surely knows he will not be able to fulfill every promise made, and who faces the worst economic crisis in half a century, inherits a tough and extremely complex job.

Another darker fear is for our new president himself. It is a fear I do not like to articulate, almost as if some childhood superstition tells me it is better left unsaid. It is the fear that some crazy person, motivated by the racism latent in every corner of this country, might hurt or kill Barack Obama. Leading up to and since the election, conservative talk radio has been rife with offensive rhetoric, some of it rising to the level of exhortation.

It's not as if the United States has been free of attacks on public officials. Most citizens tend to think of our country as above that sort of thing; it's the so-called banana republics and other third-world nations where such violence lives. Sinister forces within our own security forces murdered or facilitated and covered up the murders of President John F. Kennedy in 1963 and Attorney General Robert Kennedy and Martin Luther King five years later. Ronald Reagan survived an assassination attack. Yet most of us would still not describe our country as a place where that kind of crime can happen. Two of these men where white. Add race to the equation and the danger increases exponentially.

Within President Obama's first month in office, two incidents called particular attention to the sort of not-so-dormant racism with which we are afflicted. The first took place on February 18, 2009. The *New York Post* published a cartoon by Sean Delonas in which two New York City policemen had just shot and killed a chimpanzee. One policeman says, "They'll have to find someone else to write the next stimulus bill." Faced with an outpouring of protest, both the cartoonist and the *Post* claimed the chimpanzee in no way depicted Obama, the stimulus bill had actually been written by Congress, and, besides, they didn't think about the fact that African Americans have derogatorily been called monkeys and apes for years. All this despite the fact that in the days leading up to the cartoon's publication, Obama had pushed through his economic stimulus package and a woman had nearly been mauled to death by a friend's pet chimpanzee. Public figures of all races decried this cartoon. The *Post* was forced to issue a pale apology.

A few days later the mayor of Los Alamitos, a small town in Orange County, California, e-mailed a picture postcard to his friends. The image showed the White House lawn in brilliant color with neat rows of watermelons covering it completely. The caption read: "No Easter egg hunt this year." Mayor Dean Grose at first tried to argue that he had no idea watermelons are stereotypically linked to African American culture. He too received sharp criticism, including calls for him to resign. When he could no longer fake a plausible innocence, he did step down. I know these incidents will not be the last from racists who cannot abide the fact we now have a black president.

The very election of a president of color has roiled the racist fringe. Around this election and since, no matter how we look to statistics to analyze race and racism or anything else, incidents of this type will continue to occur. In the first year, threats against the president were 400 times what they usually are. I can only hope they will not go beyond the cartoon or postcard, and that a vast majority of citizens will continue to protest them when they surface.

Standing in stark contrast to the ugly racism this presidency has spawned are other images as well: dramatic and beautiful. I can still see that gorgeous family made up of Barack, Michelle, Sasha, and Melia, waving at a sea of supporters in Grant Park, Chicago, after Obama's moving acceptance speech. To think of that warm, grounded, intelligent, and genuine family in the White House—symbol of so much that is ugly and sterile—is moving indeed. The girls, especially, offer hope. Yet I cannot help but think as well of that other image of young black girls, murdered in Birmingham not all that many years ago. The world holds both these images in its cellular, if not in its immediately accessible, memory. In order to fully understand the meaning of today's luminous image, we must never forget its tragic predecessor.

THE CELL REMEMBERS

Walking across the many-leveled sandstone mesas—vast expanses or high narrow ledges—especially after the late summer monsoon rains, I have seen deep pockets of water reflecting the storm-dark or intense blue of sky. *Tinajas* they are sometimes called: Spanish for pitchers, or those very large earthenware jars used to keep drinking water cool and clean in shaded patios to the south.

I have come upon these natural cisterns on the high plateaus of New Mexico's Malpaís, yellow rock rising above sharp fields of broken lava that can cut right through the sole of a hiking boot. On the silent multicolored floor of Utah's Escalante Canyon system, I encountered one deep and full as a swimming hole. Unsure that if I dropped in I would be able to lift myself back over its slippery lip and out. Once, along a Canyon de Chelly trail I'd descended many times before, I turned a corner and there was one: its vulva shape unexpectedly full, holding the rain as if in sleep.

Although people think of the desert as dry, cactus and scrub brush eking their sustenance from sand and stone, those familiar with the secrets of its landscape know you can die there as easily from flood as from thirst. A lone thunder cloud may rise over a spot beyond the horizon. Only blue sky is seen. Suddenly a wall of water and mud powers through a narrow slot canyon thirty miles distant. Anyone trapped in that canyon is gone. Miles further on the deluge may spit the bodies out. In the desert water can kill or save your life.

The sudden appearance of a water pocket on otherwise parched desert can be salvation for a hiker, who falls to her knees to satiate her thirst then fills every empty water bottle: relief until the next such find. Naturalist Craig Childs has spent months searching for these pockets, mapping them, learning to understand their logic. He has discovered thousands: some in deeply sheltered spots, undisturbed for lifetimes, centuries, or longer. Others filled with rain dry to dust in a few hours or single season. These are the ones that interest me today.

Childs writes about coming upon a pool that measured about one hundred feet in length. He could see a prickly pear cactus in its depths, surrounded by *Triops* and a cloud of fairy shrimp. The cactus hadn't fallen in; it had grown there, evidence that years of drought had preceded this water. He knew that when the pool turned to dust it would retain the seeds of aquatic life for however long it takes a cactus to grow and beyond. The single-cell life forms tell their own extraordinary story.

"To survive, these aquatic-desert organisms have taken an evolutionary course that rejects mechanisms of survival used by most everything else. . . . They shrivel up until they are dry as cotton balls, releasing all of their water, entering a state known as *anhydrobiosis*. *Life without water.* Basically they die, but with the loophole of being able to come back to life."[1]

In anhydrobiosis, Childs tells us, no energy is spent. Cells turn from living structures into reinforcement material. Sensitive organs are tucked away into specialized membranes. The fascinating part of this story, repeated billions of times across the face of every desert landscape, is that if an anhydrobiotic organism's regular life span is twenty-one days and its environment dries to dust in five, even if the drought lasts for one hundred years, that span of time will be but a bleep on its biological clock. When the water returns, the organism will come into its own once more and live out its remaining sixteen days. It will remember how to keep on living and for how long.

There are many such examples of cellular memory.

Slime mold, even for those who know exactly what it is, is anything but appealing. Nor is it something that sparks most people's curiosity or that we expect to give us surprise much less revelation. But an issue of *Discover Magazine*, devoted to the hundred top scientific ideas of 2008, had something interesting to say about this single-cell organism.[2] Japanese biophysicists demonstrated that the *Physarum* slime-mold amoeba, although it lacked a brain, impressively responded to an altered environment. Not a rote response, but one clearly calculated. It may be argued that slime mold remembers.

"As the cells crawled across an agar plate the researchers subjected them to cold, dry conditions for the first ten minutes of every hour," the article reports. During these cool spells the cells slowed their motion. After three such cycles the scientists stopped changing the temperature and humidity and watched to see whether the amoebas had learned the pattern. They were surprised to find that many of the cells slowed and stopped right on the hour, obviously anticipating another bout of cold. Alternatively, when conditions remained stable for a while, the slime-mold amoebas abandoned their hourly breaks. But when another single jolt of cold was applied, they resumed the behavior, even correctly remembering the sixty-minute interval. Astonishingly, the amoebas were also able to respond to other, varying, spans of time.

Readers may reject my ascribing attributes such as calculation, measured response, variable correction, and—most especially—memory to a brainless single-cell organism. Even when we discuss the infinitely more complex human organism, the arguments for cellular memory don't convince everyone. But often this is because the promoters of acceptable theory may be unwilling rather than unable to believe something that threatens their privilege. The self-serving urge to protect one's own interests, even at the expense of truth, can be a powerful impediment to discovery and change.

For centuries it was artists, writers, and philosophers who led the exploration of consciousness and memory. The idea that experience leaves some trace in the brain goes back to Plato's metaphor of a stamp on wax; and in 1904 the German scholar Richard Semon gave that ghostly trace a name: the engram. Now science is beginning to catch up. As neuroscientists probe more deeply into brain function, memory in particular, assumptions that have held sway for many years fall away.

A recent breakthrough is the discovery of a substance called

PKMzeta, activated—so far only in animals—when cells may be described as "being put on speed-dial by neighboring neurons." This work, which scientists believe is replicated in humans, has far-reaching implications for managing memory; affecting post-traumatic stress disorder (PTSD) and addiction, even aiding in the control of Alzheimer's and other dementias.[3]

Today we know the brain is not the only site where this activity takes place. In spite of its threat to the status quo, many psychotherapists who have worked with survivors of childhood sexual abuse now believe that memory resides in other of the body's cells for as long as a person lives. Who knows if longer? In recent years the evidence has gone beyond the anecdotal and entered the serious literature. Events predating the moment at which memory is commonly studied, particularly those events producing severe trauma, live on in the cells.

Hundreds of thousands of women and men, victims of abuse from which they have disassociated or which they banished from conscious memory, have gained some measure of relief from their trauma through a technique called bodywork. This covers a variety of psychotherapies combining touch with talk, enabling the patient to access the hidden memory, work with it, and release the paralyzing tension where the experience of abuse has been stored.

I myself have experienced this rememory and release, in therapy focused on a phobia traceable to a previously unremembered experience of incest. The abuse was perpetrated by my maternal grandfather in my infancy, before I had speech and long before I had the power to protect myself.[4]

For us to emerge from the effects of traumatic abuse and be able to empower ourselves, reintegration is always necessary. And it's an ongoing process. Several contemporary thinkers, most notable among them the writer Toni Morrison, have described re-memory as a literal reconnecting of the body's discrete members, disarticulated by traumas that separated parts of us from our core self.

I also came across startling examples of such journeys when I interviewed other women. One of the protagonists in *When I Look into the Mirror and See You: Women, Terror, and Resistance*[5] is María Suárez. She and Nora Miselem were captured by paramilitary forces in Honduras in 1982. They were disappeared—a fate suffered by tens of thousands during Latin America's repressive 1970s and '80s—and held in a series of makeshift prisons where they were tortured before eventually being released. They reconnected by chance fourteen years later. I was privy to their meeting.

Among the disappeared of that time, survival was extremely rare. One of the goals of the book I eventually wrote about these two women was to explore the part they played in their own release. To this end Nora and María and I retraced their shared experience and the ways in which each subsequently dealt with her residual trauma. We spoke of the many different strategies governments and individuals use in their abuse of women, of fear, shame, and silences; and of voice, the value in claiming and inhabiting spaces of strength, the power in forging a common bond against oppression. And we spoke of mirrors, memory retrieval, gendered social messages and how these attempt to diminish or render inaccessible our natural ability to resist.

Quite apart from her prison experience, but informed by its lessons, María told a story that illustrates the power of cellular memory as well as any I've heard. "We have to learn to read our bodies," she said, "and then to trust our reactions, our impressions, our emotions. For me this has been very important, an essential recourse. I'll give you one example . . . [Some time back] I was jogging around the campus of the University of Costa Rica and a guy attacked me. His goal was rape but he didn't succeed because I was able to defend myself."[6]

María explained that she managed to get angry before she became afraid. She fought her attacker off and he fled. She then reported the incident to the police, who undertook the usual investigation. They showed her hundreds of photographs but, although she had seen the man's face, she didn't recognize him in any of them.

A year and a half later María was once again at the university making some photocopies. "I accidentally dropped some papers on the floor," she said, "and when I bent down to pick them up someone brushed my hand. I completely lost the notion of time then, the notion of where I was; everything went black. I thought I was going to pass out. At first I wondered if I had forgotten to eat lunch: it's already three in the afternoon, maybe I'm just hungry. I tried to steady myself and my reaction was so intense that the guy himself asked me what was happening, if something was wrong. I looked up and saw his face. And it was him, the man who had attacked me and gotten away."[7]

The touch of her attacker's hand against María's skin was the trigger. It awakened the memory stored in her body's cells a year and a half before. Like this story there are thousands, often explained as coincidence or disregarded because they do not easily fit our conventional notions of what memory is.

Many reject offhand the idea that memory can also reside outside the brain—even in organisms that have no brain. Once we are able to stretch our imagination to include the realization that there is such a thing as cellular memory, a number of false barriers shatter and fall.

We do not expect to find cellular memory in a shrimp-shaped desert inhabitant so small most would pass its water hole environment unaware of its existence, or in such an apparently simple single-celled organism as slime mold. Many also find it difficult to acknowledge in the highly complex cellular structure that is the human body, including but not limited to the brain.

Disrupt, invalidate, marginalize, or wreak violence upon the earth or any of its creatures, and the damage will live in memory —individual or collective—until a strategy for reinhabiting that violence is created and a means to re-member facilitated.

This is true for individual victims of what is misleadingly called domestic abuse or family violence. It is also true for torture victims, for soldiers returning from the battlefield, and for whole communities that have suffered collective horrors such as earthquakes, fires and floods, invasion and occupation, disappearance, mass rape, or genocide. The more hidden or less acknowledged the abuse, the less available emotional healing will be, and the more widespread and damaging the social consequences.

Unless and until the hideous secrets are exposed, whole groups of people—communities of different colors or beliefs, women and children who have been abused by family members, female populations targeted as sex objects or kept submissive to men, war veterans, young people victimized by the priests who pretend to befriend or mentor them—may be doomed to dysfunction by the crippling effects of what they were forced to endure.

In an effort to heal alcoholism and substance abuse, some Native Americans today are revisiting the inherited trauma of the violence perpetrated against them. In programs that differ substantially from the classic Alcoholics Anonymous model, health providers are taking people back to the sites of the old government boarding schools where Indian children were tortured for speaking their native languages or practicing their traditional ways.

Even when these people themselves didn't experience the abuse, their grandparents and great-grandparents did. The community continues to stagger beneath the weight of historical trauma. Europe's ravaging of the American Indian continues to affect subsequent generations. Only when that violence and its ongoing damage are acknowledged can healing begin. Some tribes are going back as far as the Conquest to heal the grief, shame, and hopelessness suffered by descendants this many generations down the line.

Most horrific crimes against humanity ended with vows that "this can never be allowed to happen again." To that end a broad range of strategies have been put into place, from educational programs to museums and memorials, truth and reconciliation commissions, and preventive or protective law.

Holocaust museums teach by trying to recreate in their visitors a sense of what it was like to have been victims. I remember visiting the Holocaust Museum in Washington DC. At the entrance were two small baskets, one with female IDs, the other with male versions of the same. We were asked to pick an ID appropriate to our gender and go through the museum with it in hand. In some palpable way this simple memento provided connection, enabling identification with someone not that different from ourselves who had been targeted, suffered, and died during that horrific time.

Today there are Holocaust museums in many major cities throughout the world, but still almost exclusively commemorating the Nazi extermination of Jews; others among the Nazi's victims, and other holocausts, have yet to be widely memorialized. In

Hiroshima, Japan, the monument in remembrance of that first atomic bomb dropped by the United States on a civilian population changes visitors forever. Along the West African coast, where free peoples were kidnapped and forced into slavery, their points of departure have been turned to hallowed ground. And here there are now a few interactive museums where descendants of the Middle Passage and descendants of their masters explore the heritage of slavery. Native Americans finally have a museum in Washington, and a number of tribes still work to repatriate the bones of their ancestors and sacred cultural objects as a way—among others—of healing still festering wounds.

Throughout Latin America, Europe, and Africa, survivors of more recent genocides continue to struggle with issues such as commemoration, reconciliation, accountability, amnesty, and restitution. In the wake of dictatorships and other authoritarian regimes, transitional justice remains a rich and contested field, one in which a number of human rights organizations explore the best ways for a particular people to reconcile with its abusive past and those responsible for that past. Memory, and how it is acknowledged, understood, and honored, is key. I have come to understand that these holocausts are not aberrations, but examples of how humans treat other humans over and over again. Each nation, each generation, has its holocaust. Perhaps our identities are most profoundly shaped by our relationship to it: were we perpetrators or victims, chroniclers or deniers? Did we accept or resist?

There is now no doubt that during the George W. Bush administration large numbers of innocent people were rounded up, sometimes sent to secret prisons in other countries, tortured there and here, and held for years without trial at Guantánamo Bay in Cuba, among other sites. The photographs of U.S. officials torturing prisoners at Abu Ghraib prison in Iraq shocked the world when first published. Barack Obama campaigned on a promise of closing Guantánamo. As I write, members of his own party are sabotaging that promise. It does seem likely that the notorious camp will eventually be shut down, although other prisons in other places will undoubtedly take its place. As so often happens, the symbol may fall while the policies remain intact.

An important question is if those responsible for this consistent abuse of human rights—not the few low-level scapegoats but those who made the policy—will ever be brought to accountability. It doesn't seem likely. In our current economic crisis it's all too easy to say we must "leave the past behind and concentrate on the future." But without collectively and publicly acknowledging its past, I do not believe a people can have a viable future.[8]

For life to keep flourishing, we must reconnect with memory. Now we understand that memory is accessed in many more ways than we once believed. For years brain specialists have known that the repositories and command centers for what we feel and do reside in discrete parts of the brain: specific locations developed to manage specific skills. Now they also know that when these locations are absent at birth, or damaged through illness or accident, others can often be trained to take their place.

Throughout the latter half of the twentieth century, a variety of ideas about mind and body surfaced in opposition to the more classical Freudian theories, and branched out to address problems desperately needing solution: men returning from modern wars who were crippled by shell shock and battle fatigue; an increased recognition that masses of women in very different sorts of cultures suffer domestic abuse; the abysmal distance between how we say we treat our children and how we actually treat them.

Gradually, and not without opposition, post-traumatic stress disorder (PTSD) has been added to our list of certified health problems. Although the U.S. military culture continues to ridicule and punish men who seek help for PTSD, the vast numbers afflicted by our debacles in Iraq, Afghanistan, and elsewhere are pushing the system to sit up and take notice—and, most important, grant them the services they so desperately need. Until PTSD is acknowledged and treated like any other medical disability, we will continue to have the high degree of abuse and overwhelming incidents of suicide and homicide recorded among our veterans.

Feminism cannot be underestimated here. As late twentieth-century feminist theoreticians uncovered the ways in which power abuse manipulates—indeed rules—our social structures, several psychotherapeutic schools came to understand how previously accepted power relations mask the hidden reality of widespread abuse. Despite disheartening resistance from colleagues, a few women scientists had also been exploring the issue of power. One of them, Barbara McClintock, studied slime mold in the context of her work on the genetic structure of maize. Long dismissed as "incomprehensible, mystical, even mad" by her peers, she eventually won the Nobel Prize in Physiology or Medicine in 1983—the first woman to be awarded the prestigious prize without sharing it with others.[9]

Before feminist psychologists began listening to women's stories of trauma, the abuse and protection of the perpetrators had never before been challenged. Now they began to be: first by a core group of brave women and later by broader sectors of society. When women risked speaking out about the abuse they'd suffered in silence, a tremendous social taboo began to crack. Sexual harassment in the workplace got attention, and some protective law was enacted. Incest, battery, rape, childhood sexual abuse: all these common violations and invasions of body and spirit had never really been taboo; only speaking out about them was. Once the secret was out, a more complete vision of human dignity came into being.

Within the abuse recovery movement, therapeutic schools, largely freed from ideologies developed to protect the perpetrator, began to explore cellular memory. Of course this discovery—often put forth as the ability to retrieve memories of events long forgotten—was quickly attacked by groups whose interests were threatened. Many of the kingpins of corporate America feared being unmasked: respected politicians, bank presidents, pedophile priests, the founders of country clubs. In an effort to discredit such memories, something called the false memory syndrome was invented. The False Memory Syndrome Foundation opened its door in Philadelphia, Pennsylvania, in 1992, largely influenced by an article published the year before in the *Philadelphia Inquirer*. Someone named Darrell Sifford had written questioning the long-hidden memories women were beginning to report. Eventually some of those behind the foundation were traced to the editorial boards of pornographic publications.

Today we have moved to a point where neither the violence of war nor the vast numbers of picture-perfect families hiding an ugly secret of domestic abuse are the only petri dishes where post-traumatic stress disorder grows. Modernity has pushed us beyond healthy human interaction. What is called progress may also translate as information overload, noise pollution, a cacophony of electronic devices that overwhelm even as they bring us together, and an obscene glorification of violence. Our most mundane routines can, quite literally, make us sick.

I stand still beside this rain-filled water pocket, its surface framing a reflection of rapidly moving small white clouds. The long cycle of filling and drying and filling again, organisms going to dust and remembering life, mirrors my own seven and a half decades on this earth.

I see myself.

Slime mold amoebas and anhydrobiotic organisms, anti-reductionist scientists, holistic feminists, healers who intuit the almost limitless ways in which mind and body are linked, and poets who know without knowing: all point us toward the understanding that we need an unbroken pathway back to what we have suffered in order to be able to redirect our cellular possibilities and work to make ourselves whole.

Our bodies hold vivid memories of collective and individual abuse. They are the chambers we must revisit in order to access the abuse and replay its horrors from a position of strength. We are older. We know more. We are stronger. We are no longer so vulnerable. We survive.

ROLLING EYES

These are the images that invade me as I struggle from sleep. It must be approaching dawn, maybe three or four in the morning. Hard to tell because there's no clock on my side of the bed, and I'd have to roll over and incorporate myself completely to get to my glasses. Is the pale light seeping through the high window from a full moon or the onset of day? The lush folds of canyon rock in the painting above my head are still as shadowy as the wall itself, and indistinguishable from it. I rise slowly and as quietly as I can, so as not to disturb Barbara.

This is about telling the truth or its opposite: anything from brief detour to flagrant lie. It is also about why it may be difficult to tell one from the other. Truth and lie sometimes dance with one another with such practiced grace that they appear to exchange identities. For someone like me, for whom every letter, word, person, place, and event has a color, this can be confusing.

My mother rolled her eyes, most often after a comment of my father's made in the presence of people she hoped to impress. She liked to surround herself with intellectuals, an elite clan whose accomplishments she would list as if they were her own. Dad's friends tended to be regular people, the sort who enjoyed a tailgate party before a ball game or needed a place to go on Thanksgiving. One by one Mother pronounced them unfit. Her mother, my grandmother, was a champion eye-roller; the gesture dominated almost every encounter I remember.

Eyes don't just roll; they open wide and dart upward as if in aborted flight: a negative judgment in appeal to the gods. Then the person effecting the look quickly lowers them. Or flashes them around a circle of those present, momentarily fixing them on one after another, hoping to elicit a bit of sympathetic response: a coy but knowing smile, conspiratorial sigh, or discreet nod. I don't know when the habit entered our culture or if it has always had the same significance; but it irritated my childhood and has offended me ever since.

I try never to roll my eyes. In my perception of my mother, the gesture was inextricably linked to circling around and avoiding truth.

Even when George W. Bush or Dick Cheney looked straight at the camera and declared, "The United States does not torture." Even when I read that CIA operatives in Afghanistan had been giving Viagra to local warlords in return for intelligence.[1] Even when a moment of particular drama in my favorite TV show cuts to Viagra use here at home. Or Levitra or Cialis or any one of the plethora of remedies used by virile-looking men in the throes of success to correct erectile dysfunction—reptile dysfunction, as Barbara and I have taken to calling it.

Or depression, migraines, osteoporosis, insomnia, gas, constipation, obesity, indoor or outdoor allergies (or both), high cholesterol, bad skin, arthritis, cancer, clogged arteries, or difficulty breathing. These can affect anyone, male or female, but the actors who describe their woes are almost always young and beautiful. One lie is that if we take the medication we will get better. Another is that we will look like them.

The side effects, which shouldn't worry us a bit, may be sleepwalking, fainting spells, depression, suicidal thoughts and actions (!), high blood pressure, diabetes, respiratory infection, nosebleeds, blindness or loss of hearing, some forms of cancer, and in rare cases death. "Don't drive or handle heavy machinery until you know how Ambien affects you." Try muting the sound when the list of side effects appears in small print at the bottom of the screen. Free of that commanding voice-over, it's amazing how much more ominous they loom.

Rolling dice is nothing like rolling eyes. Unless the little dotted cubes are fixed, a roll of dice is about chance. The numbers that come up decide whether the person rolling wins or loses. A roll of eyes is almost always a plea for sympathy or applause, especially when it is done by a long-suffering mother or grandmother, media pundit, or smug professor of the masculine gender as he responds to a question from a young female student. A roll of dice usually only indicates a monetary win or lose.

I don't roll my eyes, but talk back to the small screen, loudly. Rage and disgust threaten my breathing.

Death, that ultimate outcome of the monster roll of dice, definitely means something more complex these days. A friend with leukemia, facing the difficult decision of whether or not to try a mini bone marrow transplant, figured she had nothing to lose. She was right. The transplant wiped out all cancerous cells and was judged a total success, putting her on the plus side of the study being carried out by a couple of Nobel hopefuls. Two days later she died. Her body just hadn't been up for such a strenuous procedure.

Another friend, currently battling breast cancer, has been told by her doctor that the recommended postoperative treatment will most probably kill her; it could be too much for her already weakened heart. Its effect on the cancer is hopeful, though.

Rolling eyes and rolling dice—their clashing colors—have wakened me here in this bed we share, in this room, our home, this desert city where I grew up and to which I have returned, and that nurtures me now in these years of more complex contemplation. A body within a bed within a room within a home within a city within a desert landscape: all the coordinates holding me in place.

Now I've slipped from our bedroom and settle in the front of the house, in my studio, at my computer, where musings stand a chance of translating into something more solid. I never inhabit this space without renewed gratitude. So many years writing in the corners of bedrooms, on kitchen counters, eking out the time between baby feedings or after long workdays, when I was much too tired from earning a living and trying to change the world at the same time. At least my small part of it.

Growing up, I went so far as to practice in front of a mirror in order to banish the slightest resemblance to my mother and grandmother's social tics. I definitely wouldn't be caught rolling my eyes, not me. Later I was forced to adjust that vow. I wouldn't roll my eyes to set myself above or apart from any other human. My goal was not to make others feel bad.

But eye rolling may be an automatic response when faced with fabricated intelligence to co-opt the way to war, torture referred to as a mere "dunk in water,"[2] the government's distributing taxpayer money as if it were bottled water, and selling bottled water more contaminated than what comes from most faucets. Or Bush's hacks, trying to push the list of talking points to be used in reinventing his legacy. Any of these lies might get an eye roll, although my contempt is more likely to choose other forms of release.

As I age, a moment or gesture is all I need to remember a place, person, or entire chain of events. The colors help. When I think of my father, it's his hands that come to mind: thick and kind, a purplish nail or pale yellow skin-crack when weather turned cold. I recall how he reached out and closed his hands around my own in the back of an ambulance, Mexico City mid-1960s. My husband at the time had been in an auto accident and we were riding with him to the hospital. Dad's hands on mine told me everything would be all right.

I remember our holding hands again one cold night on Albuquerque's Civic Plaza. It was January 1991 and we were protesting the United States' first invasion of Iraq. This would be our last meaningful public time together; he would be gone three years later. I can still feel the warmth of his palm in that biting winter cold, and our vague irritation at Mother, who had retreated to the lobby of a nearby building to keep warm.

Later, when Dad was in the nursing home, I sometimes touched his thin forearm or tried to gentle a listless hand. Pinkish now. While he could still speak he usually told me not to. By then he had crossed into a place where touch no longer felt so good.

Of Mother I too often remember her rolling eyes. Yet there

are other, gentler, memories. Her talent for fashioning tiny gifts, "little things" she called them. The elaborate poems she wrote for birthdays, full of exuberant humor and forced rhyme. After she died I reread a few of the diaries she kept from our childhood trips, their rounded penmanship holding references to her own memories of having been somewhere before, or approval of a restaurant's delight. Once, about an eatery in São Paulo, Brazil, she wrote "the waiter's nails were clean." Often there were vivid descriptions of people or places, full of evocative detail.

My own aging and my parents' deaths have refocused a lot about how I internalize the relationship with them. Growing up, it was easy to love my father: his warm encouragement, expansive generosity, prideful loyalty; even his lies seemed truthful. Because of the nature of their relationship, part of loving Dad necessarily involved a flash of irritation at Mother, who—it seemed—used more than loved him; though who can really inhabit another's motivations?

What we knew was that she told elaborate lies to get her way. Even when they disintegrated, she would cling to them. She berated Dad's simplicity, and always wanted more than he could give. Her inability to move easily or honestly toward filling her need tended to make her devious. I was always able to love the mother I wanted more than the one I had.

Another thing about growing old is I see my parents more and more in myself. I may pass a mirror and catch sight of one of their faces—usually Mother's—where I expect to see my own, or hear her words spilling from my mouth: too late to call them back.

When my family moved west in 1947, I was ten. I alone, in our family of five, retained the New York accent. It was intentional, although it would be years before I understood why. Mother's unconscious anti-Semitism pushed her to expunge what she considered "Brooklynese" and replace it with an accent from nowhere—transparent and indeterminate, but what she thought of as highly cultured. This characterized her speech from then on. As Dad's desire was to please Mother, he came to speak much as she did. My sister and brother were too young to have retained their New York accents. I held on to mine as a desperate act of truth, an identity.

As my mother grew into the self she created, I fled in the opposite direction. I wanted to be ordinary, extraordinary, righteous, ethnic, adventurous, take every risk, defend every cause. When a relationship went bad, I left; and there were many. It would be years before I learned how much more fulfilling it can be to create a shared life than discard a broken one. When a philosophy seemed right, I lived it. Scorn became a second skin, one I am only now beginning to shed.

Truth rubbed me raw.

I learned that from truth's open wounds art is made, lives are saved, change may be possible.

Of course there are also times when the only truth is a lie: the only way of making sure the contact is made, the message gets through, the person whose life is in danger remains safe, or responsibility moves seamlessly from one set of shoulders to another. Revealing only what the other person needs to know, asking only those questions I myself need answered. Lies as perfect as the perfect poem, as powerful as dignity when no one is looking.

I discovered this kind of truth during my years in Latin America, when I chose to stand with David against Goliath. I knew those lies were as important as truth because I always felt clean after telling one.

There's also the truth that masquerades as lie because its victim has had to disassociate or "forget" in order to go on living. Abuse suffered in early childhood falls into this category. Years later, if you are fortunate, you may retrieve the memory. Then, stronger and less vulnerable, you will be able to put it where it belongs—and place yourself where you belong within your own story. I did this with my maternal grandfather's incest, and know many others who have similarly been able to replace what they believe happened with what really happened, freeing themselves in the process.

Malcolm Gladwell refers to that part of our brain that leaps to conclusions without the usual explicit steps as the adaptive unconscious. In books like *Blink* and *Outliers*, he shows how such leaps almost always reveal a deeper truth than that which may be immediately apparent.[3] This, he explains, is why intuition often leads us to a more dependable truth than labored reasoning. He doesn't refer to color.

Outside my studio window, day opens its arms to hold me. I can feel its light, even though I keep the blinds drawn: making of this place where I write completely enclosed and safe, a womblike space to which I may retreat. From the back of the house I can hear Barbara's first movements, a door opening then closing. The scent of good coffee reaches me.

Now that it's too late, I mourn the real knowledge I might have gotten from my mother, had I been able to embrace it— her truth, whatever it was. How she survived her own parents. Her early refusal to stay in school, years making art and then translating from the Spanish she was afraid to speak. The way she avoided weddings ("they usually end in divorce, so what's the point?") and funerals ("when I die, no fuss please, just give my body to medicine").

I wish I could simply have shut up, listened to the words she was able to speak, get past my own defiant interpretation. I would love to know what life was like for her, beneath the subterfuge and show. Inside the secrets. Where the pain never quite succeeded in forgetting itself.

Because years fix us in our ways, one of the marks of growing old is rigidity: truth turned inside out. Lunch at the same time every day: the same choices at the same cafeteria. A piece of furniture placed just so. The habits we cannot break. They say as we age we become more intensely who we've been. The angry become bitter, the kind more open and loving, the honest brutally so. A habit cultivated for decades is finally cast in stone.

And so I embrace age, among other things, by deliberately refusing to become a prisoner of my own idiosyncrasies. If I've worn blue for as long as I can remember, I make rusts and creams and black the new basis of my wardrobe. If I've always delighted in chocolate ice cream, I savor vanilla once in a while. The chair that for so long perfectly filled that corner of the room can just as easily grace this one.

But truth is about so much more than color or furniture.

Sometimes it hurts.

Sometimes it warms us like the sun.

Always it waits for us to catch up.

My mother rolled her eyes because she could find no other way out of the pain and tentativeness of her life. The image follows me like a warning, describing the paradox of wavering on my own steadfast journey.

REMEMBERING MOTHER

Driving past the corner of San Mateo and Roma, your balcony
is a magnet drawing my eye. Looking out, you gazed on the
mountain you loved but never climbed. Weather remained on
the far side of thick glass, windows closed through every season.
Stale smell of overcooked broccoli. Drapes powdered in dust.
Looking down, you saw the swimming pool you always said
you'd try if only you weren't so afraid of germs. And the rose
garden devotedly tended by neighbors you referred to as your
"fellow inmates."

From out here, my eyes bore through remembered walls.
Who lives there now, what festoons the current resident's space,
how does your old kitchen sink pronounce her name? Who
answers your telephone number, and where? I continue to taste

a life shedding its skin, imagine the fault lines along which it careened. We who have taken your place will also one day be done. We too will close the door, unceremoniously or with a flourish. The adverb shifts my attention to the wine-colored velvet bag at my feet, its cardboard box with your ashes.

Mother, gone almost three months now, yours was a peaceful, tidy good-bye. Sudden endgame, after almost ninety-seven years. I am surprised at how intensely I miss you. I don't really want you back, but without you my days unfold in broken cadence, awkward, off-balance. You were the reason I'm here, my brittle sounding board. Even when separated from me by definitive distance—geographic, cultural, ideological—your particular arrangement of fact and fiction signaled larger-than-life demands. A great wheel of self-doubt spun you like a top, steering you away from every risk, dropping you into crevasses from which no rescue was possible.

Yet you always knew we, or someone, would unfurl a ladder to the crevasse depth or snatch you from dangerous heights, keeping you safe another day. Superstition prevented you from voicing explicit requests, or savoring the good things for fear they might turn bad. You revisited and revised a lifetime of work, reinventing yourself in every reconfigured line. Wiping the shame from your eyes. Summer sandals strapped over feet gone puffy and purple in winter cold. Telltale coffee stains on the Goodwill blouse. And always, those lies you told so that things would go your way. The lies that justified the lies. White lies and secrets of every hue. All of them safely behind you now.

Through your last week of conscious dying, all loose ends came together in startling symmetry. Your generous smile brought us close without regret. Our single body moved about you, holding and being held by your stunning, definitive presence. For what may have been the only time, doubt disappeared, subterfuge found no place to hide. Without exception, the stream of friends who filed past your bed to say good-bye knew this woman we, your family, were meeting for the first time. We watched as your scattered pieces reassembled effortlessly, a seamless rendering of the woman you were meant to be. We circled your bed in awe of transformation, awkward gratitude for such a bacchanal of promises redeemed.

Some say the dead don't die completely until there is no one alive who remembers them. Action or response, unique arrangement of words, a particular way of marking time. Until no image remains in living consciousness, they say, those semi-dead wait in a place of semi-death. Only when no memory speaks in past or present tense do those completely forgotten enter the world of the completely dead.

Memory tells me you're still traveling.

FIRST LAUGH

for my daughter Sarah

It was on the south rim of Grand Canyon that I suddenly began thinking about laughter. Being in nature frees my brain to wander beyond city constraints. Perhaps I heard or saw someone laugh. Perhaps I was walking out along the rim when that recognizable sound invaded a relative silence in which only wind, birds, and the buzz of insects cushioned consciousness. Or perhaps I was sitting in one of the park's restaurants, where crowds share stories of recent adventure and the familiar conversational pitch would have seemed less surprising. Questions about where laughter comes from and when and how early humans first exploded with the all-consuming gesture tumbled through my mind, riveting my attention so completely I no longer remember the circumstances, only the intensity.

Why did the first humans laugh? What did their laughter mean? How was the explosive sound recognized by their contemporaries and how quickly did it become a normal part of social discourse? Was that first laugh mocking or embracing, frightening or pleasing, nervous or relaxed? Was it as contagious then as now? How many centuries would it take for nuances of satire and subversion to enter the repertoire?

How soon after its initial spontaneity did people try to provoke laughter in others? Why and how? Has laughter developed similarly in all cultures and does it really cross all cultural lines? Surely it doesn't function in the same way across classes, or mean the same to all peoples or in all situations.

How and when did ironic or bitter laughter—the clipped snort—split off from the root joy of delighted abandon? How old are we when we laugh for the first time? What physiological changes, such as the release of endorphins, take place in the body? Do animals laugh, or is laughter one of those capabilities that separate us from other primates or classes of mammals?

There are numerous and varying depictions of laughing human features, going back to the beginnings of representation. One of the most unusual—with its terrifying subtext—is the ancient Greek Gorgon Medusa, the furiously spirited female monster who struck fear into the hearts of men. Medusa had been a beautiful woman, but she angered the goddess Athena with her vanity. Athena then turned her into a Gorgon, with serpents writhing in her hair and piercing eyes that could translate a mortal to stone. In *The Odyssey*, Odysseus feared that if he stayed too close to Hades he would have to face Medusa. The French/Algerian postmodernist feminist Hélène Cixous retrieves her figure in "The Laugh of the Medusa," her 1975 essay exhorting women to move away from a phallogocentric system of language and write from the female body.[1] Patriarchal societies have long associated women with danger. I wonder if the laughing Gorgon might offer one of the earliest representations of laughter.

Increasingly, I find suspect the assumption put forth by so many so-called experts that only humans are endowed with the ability to laugh. We once had a terrier that would escape from our yard, run back and forth in front of the house, turn her head and laugh each time she passed our door. Numerous articles and TV reportages about other animals clearly show their capacity for laughter. Even a layperson like myself is able to recognize the gesture.

Superficial research tells me laughter is caused by the epiglottis constricting the larynx and causing momentary respiratory upset. And I discover that the study of humor and laughter (related although also separate) and their physiological and psychological effects on the human body has a name: gelotology.

Laughter is defined, I learn, as an audible expression or appearance of happiness. It can also be an inward feeling of joy, in which case it is sometimes described as "laughing to oneself." It starts with a smile and quickly evolves. As a physiological reaction it can be stimulated by tickling or a joke.

But this postdates by millennia the sort of laughter prodding my original question. I am less interested in the stand-up comic than in my most distant ancestor who, in her cave or pit house—suddenly responding to an unexpected change of routine or surprise—uttered some version of that spontaneous and audible physical exclamation.

If I were guided by numerology, I might look to the number seventeen for some part of the answer to these overarching questions. The number is featured in two separate sources on the subject of laughter. One describes recent research showing infants emitting vocal laughing sounds as early as seventeen days. Another claims the average adult laughs an average of seventeen times in twenty-four hours. I value humor, and silliness is an important feature of my daily interaction, but seventeen daily incidents of recognizable laughter seems like a lot.

Reading about laughter and the brain, I learn how the vocalization is linked to activation of the ventromedial prefrontal cortex, producing endorphins which in turn provoke the release of the laughing sound. Parts of the brain's primitive limbic system are also involved, suggesting laughter is an ancient activity connected to the very instinct for survival. Technical explanations that, while interesting, do little to satisfy my need to know.

An article in the December 7, 1984, issue of the *Journal of the American Medical Association* addresses the physical or neurological causes of laughter and admits that "although there is no known 'laugh center' in the brain, its neural mechanism has been the subject of much, albeit inconclusive, speculation. . . . Its expression depends on neural paths arising in close association with the telencephalic and diencephalic centers concerned with respiration." Different researchers believe this mechanism resides in different regions: the mesial thalamus, hypothalamus, subthalamus, or tegmentum. Good information but, again, not germane to the point of my inquiry.

Writers, linguists, and social scientists come closer to dealing with my curiosity. Generally they agree that laughter is a mechanism shared by everyone, part of the human vocabulary. Although there are thousands of languages and hundreds of thousands of dialects throughout the world, everyone speaks laughter in much the same way. Babies, whether at seventeen days or four or five months, laugh before they speak. Those born blind and deaf nevertheless retain the ability to make laughing sounds, and such sounds reflect a universal consciousness. Laughter is an aspect of human behavior regulated by the brain, helping people to clarify their intentions in social interaction and providing an emotional context to conversation. It is a common feature of group behavior, signaling—among much else—acceptance and positive relationships with others.

Students of human behavior conclude that a proclivity for laughter is probably at least partly genetic. There is the well-known case study of female twins separated at birth and raised by different sets of adoptive parents. In the literature they are referred to as the Giggle Twins. Robert R. Provine (who has spent decades studying laughter) reports that "each was raised by people they described as 'undemonstrative and dour.' Reunited forty-three years later, neither of these exceptionally happy women reported having known anyone who laughed as much as she did." Provine adds that "the twins inherited some aspects of their laugh sound and pattern, readiness to laugh, and perhaps even taste in humor."

We all know individuals who display a particularly frequent and/or raucous laugh, or whose actions or demeanor cause others to laugh. I have a dear friend with whom laughter characterizes our relationship. We no longer live in the same country, but when we did, and saw one another frequently, we both knew laughter would dominate our conversation. I most often played the "straight guy"; he dissolved in guffaws that brought us both to tears. Occasionally, though, my friend made me laugh as genuinely and loudly as I did him. And we both reveled in this behavior. It didn't matter if we were talking about something difficult, painful, or funny: laughter was our currency. And it became a private language with which we spoke about very serious issues.

Sigmund Freud described laughter by what is commonly called the relief theory, explaining that the action releases bodily tension and psychic energy. This and similar theories are at the root of the belief that laughter is beneficial for health ("laughter is the best medicine"), and also why it is often used in hospitals, as well, as a coping mechanism when one is angry, sad, or upset.

Many people laugh at inappropriate times—at funerals, for example, or when conveying bad news—even when the dramatic or tragic event makes such a response embarrassing. They are not laughing at the victim; rather, the gesture is automatic. Perhaps it signals a relief that they themselves are not victims. More likely it stands in for an inability to know exactly how to react.

Happiness is not the only cause of laughter. It may be provoked as well by a joke, from being tickled, or by other stimuli. Inhaling nitrous oxide (popularly called "laughing gas") can induce laughter, as can the ingestion of cannabis and other drugs. Relief, though, would seem to be the most natural cause.

And so I return to prehistory. There are many dangers, and survival means constant struggle. Relief comes as the threat of danger passes. Could such an emotion have provoked the earliest human laughter? Or was it something more intimate, the acknowledgment of a shared moment experienced in the warmth of ancient domestic life?

Inconsistency would seem to be a frequent motivator. A routine, of whatever sort, is suddenly broken by an event or words that turn the expected on end, tear at the membrane of complacency, upset the mundane, and bring surprise. This unexpected moment provokes an audible reaction.

This theory has been amply studied with regard to the art and science of humor. A joke creates an inconsistency or a sentence appears to be irrelevant—out of sync with its context—and we automatically try to understand what the sentence says, supposes, doesn't say, or implies. If we are successful in solving this cognitive riddle and understanding what is hidden within, we can bring that element out in the open. We realize that the surprise wasn't dangerous but benign, and our moment of illumination or relief brings laughter. This process is instantaneous, such that most often we do not plan it and may even be unaware it is taking place.

Comics use this rule when designing their performances. But if the inconsistency is not resolved, the comedy doesn't work. As Mack Sennett points out, "When the audience is confused, it doesn't laugh." When it "gets it," it does. Laughter can be increased and prolonged through social contagion, which is why recorded laugh tracks are often used to encourage live laughter on radio and TV. Books have been written about the history of canned laughter.

Among individual laughers there is the jester; the courts of old had one at least. Today this is often a person who hides insecurity or other personal discomfort behind a humorous façade. There is the natural comic, who may end up earning his or her living through the practice of comedy. Clowns often play this part. Even the con artist may use humor as a cover. Legitimate laughter may also have its tragic undertone. In every society he or she who laughs easily has a role to play.

Let me go back to ancient examples of laughter in the myths, stories, texts, and images that have come down to us through every cultural tradition. Medusa wasn't the only one. At least one of the artists who 30,000 years ago painted on the walls of the Lascaux caves in southern France depicted humor in his or her work. An image has been found that shows a bent-over man about to get reamed in the butt by a charging bull. Humor can be found in Egyptian hieroglyphs, Middle Eastern scrolls, tombstones and grave markers throughout time, and even in early Christian illuminated manuscripts.

We have the biblical story of Abraham and Sarah, who at one hundred and ninety years, respectively, are said to have conceived a child. They named their son Isaac, or Yitzhak, which in Hebrew means "he will laugh." Were they sharing a laugh that Abraham was still potent and Sarah could give birth at such advanced ages? Were they mocking God or themselves, expressing joy or ridicule?

Isaac himself, according to subsequent biblical passages, seems to have been a rather good-natured young man. Almost too good-natured. At the age of thirty-seven, he hardly protested when his father showed himself willing to offer him in sacrifice. If it is true that his parents were so old when he was born, perhaps he was a bit slow or even mentally retarded.

Eli Wiesel, in his *Messengers of God*, asks why the Bible's most tragic patriarch bears a name that means "he who laughs or will laugh," and suggests that perhaps the story teaches future survivors of Jewish history that one can suffer and despair an entire lifetime and still not lose the art of laughter. Many survivors of the horrors of the Nazi concentration camps—and of other genocides and holocausts—have written about humor as the best defense against the violence of repression. The Italian Roberto Benigni wrote, directed, and starred in the 1997 film *Life Is Beautiful*, which depicted life in a Nazi concentration camp. Benigni's character was a born comic who used this trait to win the love of the woman he desired. Later he must call upon this same talent to try to protect his small son in the midst of the camp's unspeakable horrors and at the moment of its eventual liberation. Audiences were divided between those who felt the appreciation of release and those for whom the use of humor in such circumstances was unacceptable.

Laughter, then, may also be linked to suffering, and vital to survival.

Some cultures, such as the Navajo or Diné, celebrate a baby's first laugh with a special ceremony. For the Diné it is A'wee Chi'deedloh. They believe a baby is of two worlds at birth: those of the holy people and the earth people. As weeks pass, adults wait and listen for the child's first chuckle, a sign of joy that signals his or her desire to join the earth community. Since the child is believed to take on the characteristics of the person who witnesses or draws forth that first laugh, unwholesome guests are kept away. At the A'wee Chi'deedloh, with adult help the child holds out salt crystals to everyone in attendance. This, the child's first act of generosity, is meant to affirm and renew each guest's good character.

Oral traditions, literature, texts of all sorts contain references to laughter and examples of it as a formal aspect of performance and response. Greek theater—indeed all theater produced throughout the ancient world, from China to Mesopotamia and Africa to the Mayan kingdoms—used laughter as prop and protagonist. Traditional theatrical masks depict comedy as well as tragedy. Sages in India used to travel the land laughing instead of preaching; inspiring their followers to laugh with them taught a lesson in the spiritual value of such physical and emotional release.

In the U.S. American Southwest, several different Indian tribes perform dances in which Mud Heads or other trickster figures provide comic relief as part of otherwise serious pageantry. Onlookers in the know laugh appreciatively. Coyote, the trickster in many Hispanic and Native stories, plays a similar role. In both cases the figures provoking laughter also teach important lessons.

Shakespearean dramas are filled with humor that has provoked ribald laughter since they were first staged. Chaucer's great accomplishment was to bring the humor of the peasantry into works such as *The Canterbury Tales*. His depiction of them mocking their oppressors was a powerful political statement. Those in power tend to laugh at, not with. In fact, satire and other forms of humor have been used throughout time to bring about social change.

In today's reductionist consumer society, humor is often used in commercial advertising to help persuade people to buy. Iconic figures and their laughter are too often reduced to roles that do nothing more than fabricate working people's need and fill the pockets of the rich.

Humor, albeit twisted rather than good-natured, has also been used by racist elements stereotyping or otherwise misrepresenting groups of people and their cultures; Al Jolson–style blackface is one example. Following Barack Obama's election as our first African American president, racists have tried to justify their ongoing attacks by pretending they are harmless jokes.

All this, though, seems largely irrelevant to my quest—except as it may illustrate the range of fallout from the original laugh.

In a layperson's terms at least, I understand the physical manifestations of laughter: what bodily impetus initiates it and how it is expressed. I am familiar with the ways in which laughter has been used in literature and theater, its place in a variety of cultures, how it manifests itself in my own life and those around me, and the various theories that have emerged to explain its many functions. I myself have laughed so hard I have wet my pants, suffered long bouts of hiccups, or experienced physical pain.

What still evades me is that very first human interaction in which something happened and someone laughed. It seems probable that an interruption of consistency was the cause. But what constituted consistency back then? Can we probe that long-lost era? Can we even imagine it? Is there any way of removing ourselves from all that we've experienced and learned, such that we may glean intuition regarding that first laugh?

Why does laughter intrigue me today, so much more than lying or greed, fear or anger, comfort or cunning?

I don't know. But I long to be able to retrieve that moment lost to time, that instant in which for the very first time someone did or said something, someone else laughed, and then perhaps others joined in. Might a different value placed on laughter, a different respect for its complex powers of levity and release, have changed the course of history? Could laughter have avoided our descent into violence, the wars that engulf us now? Is it even possible to guess?

PIERCING THE WALLS

for my son, Gregory

The Great Wall of China, the Berlin Wall, the wall Israel is
building to contain the Palestinians, or the wall between Mexico
and the United States—currently advancing in blustering incre-
ments of hate across our southern border. Sometimes called
curtains: as in Iron Curtain, Bamboo Curtain, or El Telón de
Azúcar (Sugar Curtain), the term some Cubans use to describe
the isolation of their island this many years after successfully
rejecting foreign domination. Diplomatic, trade and military
blockades, misinformation and lies, fear, abuse, and prejudice:
all make barricades effective for the walls' builders while dangerous and isolating for those kept in or out.

The kidnapping and sale of human beings, the slave ships of
the Middle Passage, and the germ-infested blankets of the white

man's wars against Native peoples—tragedies all, some reaching the definition of genocide—have become metaphors as well, separating the experience of the ravaged from the perpetrator's crime. This difference splits cultural roots, shaping the histories of the conquerors and those of the conquered in ways that may never heal. Slave labor, devastation of families, removal from ancestral lands including those where family members are buried, forced marches, stock reduction: despite the fact that some of us descend from one of these histories and some from another, Empire's version of them all is what informs our consciousness. No accident, of course. Silencing itself is a wall as well as a weapon.

Now, through necessary historical rectification, we can understand how those human auction blocks and germ-infested blankets in effect represented walls between the colonizers and the colonized—and successive generations of their progeny. Atrocity always requires silence. Fear and a fabricated shame make silence possible. The Armenian Holocaust is still the subject of reluctant mention today; almost a century beyond its perpetration, few are able or willing to speak of its horrors. Recently Turkey and Armenia renewed efforts to heal this wound between their nations. Progress remains hesitant at best. Once such events pass into a biased historical record, ignorance and attitudes of trivialization, disregard and fear of difference, reinforce the distortion of memory.

Poets, writers, artists, scholars, and thinkers everywhere are called upon to retrieve this memory, break these silences.

Hitler's concentration camps, where six million Jews and thousands of Communists, Roma, homosexuals, and others deemed "imperfect" met barbaric death, remain the iconic symbol of twentieth-century criminality, one that continues to set the horrific standard and also, sadly, has sometimes been used as an excuse for later crimes. (I think of those Jews who migrated to Israel, where they hoped to find a safe haven even as they grabbed territory and established new boundaries that ravaged their brother and sister Palestinians, for whom that land is also sacred and who have lived upon it for centuries.)

As I began writing these notes, I came upon an article from the Associated Press dated April 15, 2008. It tells the story of Marek Edelman, then the only survivor among the four commanders of the 1943 Warsaw Ghetto uprising. Now he too is gone. Two hundred twenty scrappy, poorly armed boys and girls, between the ages of thirteen and twenty-two, resisted the Nazi army determined to exterminate an entire Jewish ghetto of 400,000.

Before he died, Edelman told this story: "I remember them all, not too many to remember their faces, their names. When you were responsible for the lives of some 60,000 people, you don't abandon their memory." By his annual remembrance, sixty-five years later he continued to give lie to the repeated claim that the Jewish people didn't resist. His was one in a growing fabric of memory strands that helped to decimate walls of forgetting. Memory—preserving it, placing it front and center, honoring it so those who are born when everyone who participated in a precious moment are gone—may be the best resistance against the erection of walls.

Despite repeated pleas that these travesties must never be allowed to happen again, Cambodia's Killing Fields, Ireland's Catholics and Protestants set against each other for generations, two decades of Latin American Dirty Wars, and the contrived rage pitting Rwanda's Hutus against Tutsis are but four examples of subsequent crimes against humanity—and I limit myself to those in the twentieth century.

Fear and mistrust make the strongest walls of all. Walls that keep out and walls that contain, spawning a hatred that diminishes those on both sides. Silence, cowardice, and conformity keep the walls standing. Our challenge is to pierce these structures, give voice to memory, revive and reignite history. A single voice may inspire a chorus.

Colonialism and neocolonialism's arbitrary divisions create walls of unimaginable profit, pathos, and loss: Koreans separated by the imposition of their country's division into North and South, Vietnamese for so many years kept apart at the seventeenth parallel. In 1974, just six months before the Vietnamese victory, I traveled to North Vietnam. I was one of only nine foreigners in that country at the time. My guide was a middle-aged woman who had been active in the resistance in the south and at the moment of division was on a mission in the north. As we walked across the bridge leading to the liberated zone of Quang Tri, we held hands. Tears spilled from her usually stoic eyes. It was the first time in twenty years that she would set foot in the south, where her only daughter had remained in 1954. She knew we would be nowhere near where she last saw her daughter, couldn't even know if she was still alive (all communication had been cut). But the symbolic closeness was enough to shatter her proud composure.

Today this tragedy is repeated among Cubans living on the island and their family members who emigrated, between immigrants from a dozen Latin American countries whose labor is needed in the United States but whose families are not welcomed here. Immigration reform has remained a thorny issue for both U.S. political parties through a succession of administrations.

Surely one of the great ironies of the late twentieth and early twenty-first centuries is the enormity of migration: not walls but their opposite. Literally millions of displaced, homeless, hungry people walk toward a diminishing hope: Guatemalan families escaping hundreds of razed villages, the Lost Boys of Sudan, pitiful parades of refugees from Darfur and other scenes of unrelenting violence. My generation retains images of those displaced by World War II, as well as the knowledge that those European refugees were ultimately cared for by international organizations and most eventually returned to their homes. Today's migrants exist in numbers too vast for any organizational solution. They will likely die or remain in camps for the duration.

The partition of India and Pakistan. Kashmir's high-altitude pain. Today's Iraqi borders, drawn by men in European seats of power, ignorant and unconcerned about how their maps would affect peoples with shared cultural roots, language, customs, family, and desire. Today we have learned at least some of those divisions can actually be traced to mistakes: a simple misunderstanding here, a bit of drunken carelessness there. Error piled upon arrogance in a brutal history of violence and manipulation. Walls drawn on documents of conquest and erasing the everyday memories of people on the ground.

And of course one of the scenarios that claims our agonized attention today: the U.S. invasion and occupation of Iraq, years now and ongoing. It may be the most horrendous example of a war based on lies and denial, unpopular even in the country of its perpetrators. To date it has cost more than a million Iraqi and some five thousand U.S. lives—to say nothing of those tens of thousands more on both sides who have been uprooted, displaced, impoverished, traumatized, and often turned into helpless killers. More than any previous such travesty, the U.S. war in Iraq exemplifies the will of a few having their criminal way despite all manner of protest. Here we witness a wall of arrogance we have yet to effectively pierce. The U.S. invasion and occupation of Afghanistan is of increasing concern as well, nine years old now and rising front and center as the mainstream press abandons Iraq.

Right here, inside our own country, we have a gnawing example of devastation, forced migration, ineptitude, and lack of official regard. I am speaking, of course, about the victims of hurricanes Katrina, Rita, and Ike, many of whom years after those storms hit have given up on their government's broken promises, insurance company denials, or anyone's apology. Surely the wall that separates the impoverished and mostly black parishes of New Orleans from its upper-class neighborhoods is obvious to anyone who cares to look. It is a wall constructed of disdain, abandonment, failure to come to the aid of a dying people, fallacious mischaracterization, and scams perpetrated by government agencies and the private sector alike. And it is a wall that did not result from the damage of those storms but preceded them by generations. It goes back to the racist attitudes and policies that kept a poor, mostly black population in the low-laying areas while the wealthier whites remained safe on higher ground.

Today these walls still stand. Inadequately repaired levees are incapable of resisting a category 5 hurricane. New Orleans survivors remain separated and scattered throughout the country, the city has been reshaped to favor a whiter, wealthier population, block upon block of rotting houses are still boarded up, and historic neighborhoods remain uninhabitable. The Bush administration turned its back on our country's Gulf Coast while at the same time having the gall to single out Burma's dictators as unresponsive to their people's needs when violent storms assailed that country. Obama's discourse has been better, but to date no real solution for the peoples of the Gulf Coast has been forthcoming.

Our prisons are also real and metaphorical walls that daily destroy the integrity of our society. More people per capita are incarcerated in this country than in any other, and the percentages of our various social groups are heavily weighted on the side of the poor and people of color. Building and running new prisons is one of our fastest-growing industries. Rehabilitation is mostly a sham.

All these walls are traced on maps, which shift with new national splits and occupations but basically continue to reflect Empire's vision. Maps, since their inception, have been used as tools of misrepresentation, disparagement, denigration, and conquest, erecting arbitrary walls in conquest's wake. Chellis Glendinning tells us that "empire originates in the perception of place" and "maps are the tools of that perception." In her profoundly moving book *Off the Map*, she analyzes some of the ways in which she and all of us receive not simply a neutral education but one designed to reproduce "the perception, thinking and body language of a citizen of empire."[1]

In 1569 the Flemish cartographer Gerardus Mercatur published the first modern *mapus mundi*, detailing the world as it was then known: the entire round sphere with poles and the equator, depicting oceans, land masses, and all the different countries in relation to one another. The first European explorations of the New World had been undertaken not too many years before. Empires, striking out in the name of God and greed and voracious of further possession, wanted to document their holdings and what they might yet claim. This map is still used in most classrooms, international institutions, and news reports today. The only changes that have been made respond to further national redistribution emerging as various countries fight for primacy, winning here, losing there.

Mercatur saw the world from his sixteenth-century Eurocentric perspective, one in which the era's science, mathematics, politics, even the capabilities of its machinery of knowledge reproduction, determined the cartographer's designation. Guided by longitude and latitude, he stretched lines to create equidistant divisions, such that the further one got from the equator the more distorted the lines became.

Mercatur placed Europe at his map's center. The north became larger, the south smaller. Europe ended up being much more prominent than it is, and the United States, for example, appears larger than Brazil, which, in reality, covers many more square miles. The nations we refer to as the Third World—dependent nations of mostly dark-skinned peoples—all appear smaller and less significant than the nations engaged in their conquest. Way up in the arctic north, the land mass appears thirty-six times its actual size. There is no acknowledgment of this. The distortion takes up residence in our worldview, affecting how we understand what is. Herein are the roots of the North's designation of a global South.

Of course, a sphere represented on a flat piece of paper cannot but contain distortion. This is understandable, and in an ideologically just world might be easily explained, even remedied. Our world wasn't rooted in justice back in Mercatur's time and it isn't today. The problem with Mercatur's map, more than the false dimensions of each country or continent, is the relationship between those areas portrayed as falsely large and those shown as unrealistically small. This proportional misrepresentation creates and maintains walls that invade our thinking, the way we see

ourselves and others, propitiating an arrogant sense of entitle-
ment in those whose countries are represented as oversized.

Even when an alternate cartography has developed—the
Peters Projection and several others come to mind—Mercatur's
colonialist imaging defines our world. It continues to keep in
place our overarching walls. Who, after all, defines what is up?
As the Arab American cultural critic Edward Said has written,
"Today's empire is the global economy."[2] Today, when we speak
of globalization, we are speaking of the logical consequences
of the geopolitical, economic, and social vision Mercatur gave
us almost half a millennium ago. Its world image is imprinted
on our DNA.

Beyond borders, our whole understanding of a living earth—
and the human-provoked climate change that threatens life
as we know it—can be traced to this same greed-based view
of weather and accountability, or lack thereof. Unimagined
advances in technology abet this view. Misrepresentation and
misunderstanding are as close as the Hollywood blockbuster,
nearest television screen, school curriculum, computer, cell
phone, Web site, blog: cyberspace's whole ever-expanding web.
We depend, among other elements, on our human heart, a creative sensibility, courageous scholarship, and the poet's primal
voice to pierce the walls, recover or redesign possibility, redirect
technology, nourish—indeed save—life.

I do not want to talk about these geopolitical walls without
speaking as well of the more intimate walls constructed within
families, social and religious bodies, and between generations, by
unacknowledged greed, power inequality, and abuse. The wall
between the patriarchal, self-serving, and power-crazed adult and
the helpless child, victimized through incest or other forms of
abuse, is one that may last a lifetime. The husband who abuses

his wife, parents who mistreat their children, clergymen who take advantage of their parishioners: these so-called personal assaults mirror the walls between nations, imposed by invasion and occupation. And those more publicly acknowledged walls, in turn, mirror those kept within the hidden crevices of family and community. Such walls are more alike than is generally understood. The line supposedly separating the intimate from the public or global is more permeable than we imagine. And the same courageous voice may pierce both.

Walls can be deceptive. Because time is not always linear, and no building material is entirely immune to the penetration of the human spirit or body's cellular memory, walls can be eroded by memory retrieval or disintegrate beneath the weight of need. We can tear them down and raise them up in unexpected ways and within the creative spaces we ourselves design. Communication of one sort or another can be traced to the very origins of life. Poetry, the most distilled and richest form of communication, crosses a magical line, entering a field where astonishment lives. It is charged with causing our bodies to tremble, our minds explode. It can reveal what has been hidden, retrieve balance, safeguard justice, inspire peace. Today, especially, it is a remedy to be taken seriously.

An opposing image to that of the wall—real or metaphorical— might be that of the road, path, or bridge. Talking stick or singing wire. Troubadour. Carrier pigeon. Whispered message. "From my mouth to God's ear."

Through centuries before our era, the Silk Road—splitting as it headed north or south—carried ideas and sensibilities as well as goods for barter or trade through precisely those parts of our world being ravaged by imperialist greed today: Afghanistan, Lebanon, the Sahara and Syrian deserts, Levant, and ancient Constantinople. Place names still salty on our lips: Persia, Mesopotamia, the Indian subcontinent. Five thousand miles of traders, merchants, pilgrims, monks, soldiers, nomads, and urban dwellers pushed forward in a constant movement of enrichment and exchange. At Petra the Nabataeans offered the sustenance of water in exchange for implements, rare metals, and spices; the arrangement built an empire that didn't require violence to consolidate its power.

Much earlier, the Bering Straits became a road for migrations of ancient peoples moving south. It is interesting to consider for a moment that nomadic peoples neither defended privacy of place nor competed for power. Walls did not yet exist. There were the stone roads along which runners carried fish from the sea to the Inca highlands of Peru. Food and messages. And roads that extended life and its creative force, like those broad straight avenues moving out in the four directions from Chaco Canyon in New Mexico, linking outlier communities to the Great Houses our ancestral Puebloans inhabited from the eleventh to thirteenth centuries. Roads that connect. Pathways of energy and knowledge.

Pathways of wisdom, arcs and continuums of connection. Literature, mathematics, science, music, and spirituality. Books endemic to every culture, written and read in every language. Figures chipped into rock, painted in alcoves spanning millennia. Images we cannot decipher but whose power rivets us nonetheless, often signaling pathways back to ourselves. Lines forming figures or designs visible only from the sky: Peru's Nazca lines and the crop circles of northern Europe. And natural clefts and faults in the earth's crust, like the rift that splits Africa from south to north, continental divides that part waters and send rivers flowing in opposite directions, seaways that guided the peoples of the South Pacific with only stars and wind for maps.

Today's examples may be more virtual than real: cyberspace information highways, by which we are instantly linked to people thousands of miles away, can send and receive words and images, rally idea and action, exhortation and lament. These electronic pathways propel us forward. I want to believe we can use the ever-evolving technology for life instead of death, that cyberspace may one day bring us closer together rather than broaden the gulf between rich and poor (the One Laptop per Child initiative is an important start). But I am also aware of the danger implicit in the control of these technologies. Who owns cyberspace? We must continue to nurture some of the slower, more tactile and human means of communication as well. A meditative stillness. A hand on the shoulder. A slow caress. Faster is not always better. More is so very often less.

Our words, our poems, are bridges linking memory to energy, the natural elements to our waving hands, revelation to a mind burdened by noise and lies, a piercing streak of light to a heart in trouble. Connection embraces, engenders, propagates. The bridge may be electronic, spoken, or embossed upon the page with the oldest printing method known. Slowing down is always an option. "No ideas but in things," as the great William Carlos Williams observed, and although the line might seem to privilege product over process, I believe the poet was asking us to look at the places where object, idea, and use converge—and how.

I urge us to navigate and look past the roadblocks those who would control us place in our way, to explore our authentic experience in the development of a language that risks, embraces, and propels; in designing actions that put people before profit and redress social wrongs. I urge us to resist and reject the cooptation of language bombarding us daily through a sold-out corporate media, rigged "scientific studies," lying commercials, and the empty verbiage that passes for public discourse. Even the academy is not immune to these distortions; often, because it has become so dependant upon Empire for recognition and funding, it may in fact perpetrate them.

One of Empire's most devious and implacable weapons is memory erasure. As it robs us of our histories it fills our minds with seductive images, inserting us into a dangerous program in which we become the malleable pawns the system requires to consolidate its concentration of power. In this way we are coerced into acting against our own best interests. Memory is erased by false stories, by social manipulation and battering, even by incessant noise. Today's proliferation of noise—its sheer decimal volume—drowns out the voice within, the doubts, the alternative choices. We must learn the difference between power and empowerment.

Recent years have seen a great deal of important work in the area of memory. Oral history has developed as a genre in which the protagonists of events have been able to tell their own stories. And so certain histories have been rewritten, although their accessibility too often follows the fad of the moment. Language outside the mainstream is sometimes honored, like stream of consciousness or automatic writing, Black English, Spanglish, hip-hop, dream. Feminist therapy has encouraged the retrieval of sexual and other abuse memories, helping many women and some men to begin their journey to healing. These, too, are vital pathways, piercing walls. This work has also opened us to the reality of cellular memory, making possible certain stunning connections.

I have found particularly relevant the idea that the invasion of a woman's or child's body by someone in a position of power, and the invasion of a small country by a larger, more powerful one, have a great deal in common. Both are rooted in the need to conquer. Both make use of violence and coerce through lies and manipulation. Both provoke strikingly similar damage in their victims. Only the scale is different.

In the years following the American war in Vietnam, more veterans took their own lives than died in combat. The wars in Iraq and Afghanistan—the so-called wars on terror—are already producing overwhelming numbers of men and women doomed by PTSD. The suicide statistics have intentionally been covered up, but the numbers beginning to emerge are staggering. An increase in domestic violence is another result of sending people off to kill and then expecting them to readapt when they come home. A recent report tells us two out of every five U.S. military personnel fighting or returned from these wars suffer a crippling form of PTSD.

During my generation, some of us have sought change and empowerment in political revolution. In the years immediately following the 1989-90 disintegration of the socialist bloc, many of us suffered a collective depression. Our very identities seemed in jeopardy. But our goal of an equitable division of power remains just, and many of our gains continue to shape us today, or to establish standards to which we may continue to aspire. We must resist the urge to see nothing but failure in the fact that we did not achieve our goals.

We did make the mistake of believing economic justice would bring with it all other forms of justice; that race and gender equality—respect for difference—would be achieved once the class war was won. Because we weren't able to braid the rights of women, people of color, and other relegated groups in the struggle for a better society, many of the old equations continued to plague us. The sexually "different," the mentally and physically othered, weren't considered at all. Power essentially passed from one dominant group to another, accompanying varying degrees of (always partial) social change.

Some of us looked to feminism, a philosophical stance that goes quite a bit further in speaking to us about the nature of power itself. Feminism, at its root, is a new way of looking at power, and a practice that stresses empowerment. But almost everywhere patriarchy defines traditional roles, and it has not been difficult for the capitalist system to distort and denigrate feminist ideologies. The notion that feminism is dead, or that this is a "postfeminist" era, is one more of Empire's inventions to keep us submissive. And the idea that feminism is a reflection of bourgeois conditioning that can divide the working class is an invention of certain quasi-revolutionary movements, used to keep their male leaders in power. A feminist analysis of power divisions is absolutely necessary to the creation of new forms of struggle.

But we need more.

Some have given up entirely on the more secular philosophies and turned to a variety of spiritual practices for clues to effecting change in our communities and ourselves. Positive values exist in a number of these, but the hierarchical structures of most religious configurations also tend to perpetuate power inequalities, to privilege stagnant constructs, and to dull the individual's capacity to question and explore. I believe one of the greatest dangers in today's world is the explosion of religious dogma put forth as policy. The fundamentalist stratum in every one of the world's major religions distorts and threatens healthy relationships between individuals, family members, communities, and nations. Today, Christianity and Islam, in particular, are locked in a holy war of terror and annihilation. Walls rise ever higher.

Still, there is more than the science story. The Hopi story. The Navajo story. A thousand different stories in which peoples of every culture bring themselves from their beginnings and take themselves home. I walk across a desert landscape listening for the song of the canyon wren.

Recognition of and respect for difference is key. Empire's troubling race, class, and gender issues would not exist if we could see each person and group as a unique part of a healthy and creative whole. Patriarchy, greed, xenophobia, white supremacy and other forms of racism, heterosexism, and capitalism construct the walls of fear that make this so difficult. It is up to us to break down the walls—in our lives, our relationships, and our work.

I want to close by speaking of several initiatives aimed at building bridges where walls once stood. One of these has risen from the ruins of one of the starkest divisions in modern history, the splitting in two of Europe symbolized and embodied by the Berlin Wall. It's been twenty years since it came down, not because Ronald Reagan pompously demanded, "Mr. Gorbachev, tear down this wall!" but because peoples throughout Berlin and all of Europe were ready to pierce it. We all know the subsequent history: thousands of joyous family reunions followed by the slow and painful reintegration of two very different social systems. Less well known, outside the immediate vicinity, is the effort to turn the once barren and militarily controlled strip between East and West into a place of conservation and regeneration, one that stands as a model for what may one day be possible in other places where walls now divide: between the two Koreas, along the U.S.-Mexican border, and between Israel and Palestine, to name just three.

Dr. Kai Frobel, a German ornithologist and conservationist, grew up in the shadow of the Iron Curtain. From the small West German village of Hassenberg, he lived only about four hundred yards from the Bavarian border with the East. Between the two heavily fortified fences was the heavily mined "death strip." From his teenage years Frobel was an avid birder, uninterested in politics. He could not have imagined the fall of the Soviet Union nor a future removal of the restrictions that kept peoples separated but proved no obstacle to birds. As Frobel grew and observed, he took stock of an interesting phenomenon. Along that part of the strip not kept barren by militarization, something astonishing was happening. During the wall's thirty-seven-year existence, off-limits to industrial farming with its poisonous fertilizers, a wide swatch of land gradually became a paradise for threatened species of birds, mammals, insects, and plants. Life was flowering in the shadow of separation and death.

Bird lovers on both sides of the wall began to make contact with each other. Change arrived and in December of 1989, only a month after the wall came down, conservationists on both sides met to hammer out a plan that would lead to the creation of Europe's largest and longest permanent nature reserve. The green belt now stretches along the length of the former Iron Curtain from the Baltic to Bavaria's borders with the Czech Republic. Frobel says, "The aim is to turn the Iron Curtain's entire 4,250-mile length—extending from the Arctic to the Black Sea—into what is already being called the Central European Green Belt."[3]

Others are building innovative bridges along our southern border with Mexico. Sound sculptor Glenn Weyant has embarked upon what he calls the Anta Project. In southern Arizona he has been playing the fence with a cello bow, holding a contact mike to the vibrating construction material, and now has several hours of four-track sound that convey the memory of division humanized by one man's creativity. In southern California priests and ministers offer communion wafers through the chain-link fence. Members of families split by cruel immigration policy can sometimes be seen playing volleyball with a low section of the wall as their "net." And numerous photographers are documenting the travesty and resistance along what poet and philosopher Gloria Anzaldúa called *una herida abierta*, "an open wound." Vision, courage, and creativity are required to make these transformational statements.[4]

Nation states have mostly failed in their attempts to heal divisions, stop climate change, end war, or save the earth. Margaret Mead famously said, "Never doubt that a small group of thoughtful committed people could change the world. Indeed it is the only thing that ever has." Let us join the Frobels and Weyants to imagine our walls into gardens, habitats, and connection.

How Much Coyote Remembered

O, not too much.
And a whole lot.
Enough.

SIMON ORTÍZ

OÑATE'S RIGHT FOOT

We are driving through Las Cruces, southern New Mexico, on
our way to the small community of Mesilla, once the largest
and most important stop along the early San Antonio–Los Ange-
les wagon route. Lots of pioneer history here, deep traditions,
meaningful stories. Today Mesilla oscillates between some two
thousand regular inhabitants and up to ten thousand when the
yearly Border Book Festival or other events take place. Mesilla
is lovely, a little *biscochito* of Hispanic heritage and pride. Old
adobes line its pretty square and continue for several blocks in
every direction.

Some have called this village the Santa Fe of the south, or
another Santa Fe in the making, descriptions that seem spe-
cious to me. Mesilla has neither Santa Fe's sophistication (in

the best sense of the term) nor such a catastrophic gap between the very rich and those who serve them. It is what it is: a sweet and inviting village with deep Mexican/American roots. Perhaps where it most resembles Santa Fe is not in what it may one day become but in what it has been for centuries: a community of old and deeply rooted Hispanic heritage.

I begin this essay in this way because I believe all cultures have value, and the people who came from Spain via Mexico to New Mexico brought much that still distinguishes them: religious tradition, music and art, unique foods, rich language and values. The Crypto-Jews, Spaniards who escaped the Inquisition and whose descendants remain in the northern part of the state, continue religious and cultural practices that are still being uncovered. All of us must learn to discern what is true and valuable in our heritage, and in those of others. There is much to celebrate.

If we care about all peoples, though, we must also pay attention to what is worth preserving and what is ugly: what we should remember only so we can effectively prevent a repetition of its poison. In our various indigenous cultures, in our Hispanic or Latino cultures, whether of Asian, African, or European origin, all of us face this challenge. It is up to each of us to face it humbly and with respect for others.

As we approach Mesilla, I find myself face to face with a large sign advertising Oñate Plaza. The name's obscenity takes me by surprise. As far as I know, I have no Indian roots. But as a human I am suddenly nauseous, revolted, and angry. Couldn't the local inhabitants have thought of a forebear more worthy of giving name to this small shopping mall than the sixteenth-century war criminal?

In fact, Don Juan de Oñate's name adorns plazas, malls, schools, and public buildings all over the U.S. American Southwest. The University of New Mexico has an Oñate Hall. As I write, Oñate Elementary School in Albuquerque is in the local news. Its students and teachers are talking about violence, how to identify and prevent it: a worthy project. But the irony seems invisible to the school as well as to many in the community; if we have not been educated about the names we use and revere, we cannot know our history, make the necessary connections to our lives, or be selective about what we want to preserve or discard.

Don Juan de Oñate was a second-rate conquistador. Among the sixteenth-century adventurers, myths of glittering cities of gold had long since faded, and Spain wasn't underwriting expeditions by mavericks. Some say Oñate never set foot in Europe, much less visited the Spanish Court. Unlike the crown-sponsored expeditionaries—Columbus, Cortéz, De Soto, Coronado, Cabeza de Vaca—he was neither funded nor sent expressly by the monarchy. But in northern Mexico he became infatuated with the dreams of conquest rampant in his time—and ours. His father had discovered and exploited some of the richest silver mines around Zacatecas. The young Oñate chose a different route. He underwrote his expedition with family money and donations he was able to raise.

This is the history of Oñate in New Mexico. During the cold New Mexican winter of 1598, a small group of Acoma Indians lived peacefully some sixty miles west of what we now call Albuquerque. For as long as they could remember, the community had inhabited this land of multicolored rock, yellow sandstone cliffs, wild sunflowers, and great open skies. Their ancestors had come from the north, from Chaco and Mesa Verde. They spoke Keresan and still do. At Acoma, atop first one glittering mesa and then another, they built stone homes with windows of mica to let in the clear desert light. The wisest among them made decisions from within their kivas. They cultivated corn and beans. All Native Americans shared their resources. Land was communally owned. When the Europeans came, they were shown hospitality and treated with respect—until their murderous intentions became clear.

As 1598 neared its end, this peaceful life was suddenly torn apart. In April, Oñate and his men, along with a group of Franciscan Friars, had set off from Zacatecas in search of gold. They bore arms and the Christian cross: symbols to this day of invasion, occupation, and death. When they reached the Rio Grande, they celebrated mass. With the rhetoric typical of the times, Oñate formally declared all lands north of the river to be under Spanish rule and all peoples inhabiting those lands subjects of the Spanish Crown.

Just as today's criminals avoid mentioning oil when seeking to justify their invasions and occupations, *La toma* (literally, "The Takeover")—the Spanish document of April 30, 1598—did not mention the search for gold, but rather the salvation of a people by taking their land and forcing their conversion to Catholicism. Christianity was touted then much like Democracy today; when an invading force imposes what it believes to be a superior way of life, all manner of devastation is excused. Gold didn't have to be explicitly mentioned in that document. Rumors of its existence attracted the Spanish to what today is the southwestern United States just as four centuries later Middle Eastern oil would put a glint in George W. Bush's eye.

In December of 1598, white men in leather and steel accompanied by others in long dark robes rode up to the Acoma mesa on horseback. I don't know if they forced their steeds up the rocky rise or dismounted and climbed on foot to the village.

This band of Spanish conquistadores didn't come in friendship. Their mission was to claim the land and its resources, enslave the people—mutilating or murdering them when they refused to surrender—and impose the religion that acted as such a useful mechanism of control.

Emboldened by a racist sense of superiority, deceit, gunpowder, and insatiable greed, the invaders raped and plundered with total disregard for the ancient belief system and communal harmony that had served the Indians for generations. Modern-day Acoma people still bear the emotional scars of this assault. A collective post-traumatic stress is written into their DNA. But resistance also figures prominently in this story. Although the Acoma were conquered by surprise, trickery, and superior weaponry, and although most now practice Catholicism, what is apparent to the outsider and those rituals observed in private differ significantly. Public ceremonies combine a mixture of Christianity and traditional belief, while the sacred ceremonies remain indigenous.

Faced with their attackers' superior technology, the people of Acoma devised their own defense and succeeded in protecting their village. A number of Oñate's men were tossed off the 300-foot-high mesa, dying on the jagged rocks below. When the people resisted, in a battle in which some thirteen soldiers were killed—among them Oñate's nephew—the invaders retreated and regrouped. They withdrew to Mexico but returned the following year, vowing to take the village and surrounding territory.

The 1599 siege lasted three days and, according to the Spanish themselves, more than eight hundred men, women, and children were butchered. Many males had their right foot severed. Of those whose lives were spared, young men and women between the ages of twelve and twenty-five were enslaved for twenty-five years. Sixty young girls were sent to Mexico City, never to be heard of again.

Back in Mexico, following his exploits in the north, Oñate was tried for his excessive abuses at Acoma, fined a large sum of money, briefly imprisoned, and banished forever from the occupied territories. His titles were taken from him. He would never again gain favor with the Spanish Court nor be allowed to take part in the conquest. He ended his days as a mining inspector, accompanied only by his personal memories of misadventure. Even for that time in which conquest itself was unchallenged, Oñate's brutality was considered out of line.

Whether from the Old or New World, and although scant historical documentation exists, there is no doubt about Oñate's intentions. He was an opportunist who sought honor, a title, and the riches successful conquest could bring. In the late sixteenth century the way to achieve all this was by leading an expedition north and claiming land and peoples for the Spanish Crown and Cross.

Despite this sad history, in recent years several exuberant monuments to the memory of this mercenary have been erected in the U.S. American Southwest. In my own Albuquerque, interest in Oñate was revived over the last several years in the run-up to the city's tercentennial celebration in 2006.[1] Not content with commemorating the Spanish Duke of Albuquerque or other less controversial figures, the event planners thought nothing of celebrating the sixteenth-century criminal. Debate, however, was anything but even-handed. Despite a 2004 poll by the *Albuquerque Journal* showing that 73 percent of those queried objected to honoring the man, the project went ahead.

The area's first large Oñate statue was erected near Española in 2002, in the small northern New Mexico town of Alcalde.

The site was chosen because the conquistador had once made his home there. The bronze was originally placed outside a community building. Perhaps those who erected it thought it would increase civic pride and improve people's lives. Taxpayer money in the amount of $1.2 million was used to underwrite the memorial.

When a brave protestor sawed off that statue's right foot, as a way of memorializing the flesh-and-blood feet Oñate ordered cut from Acoma males in 1599, it was moved inside. Subsequently, because so few people visited, it was taken back out. Currently it stands on the main road where it can't be missed. Ten thousand dollars more was spent on repairing the damaged foot and another twelve thousand to cover the cost of the various site changes.

According to the Acoma artist and activist Maurus Chino, the Alcalde center pulls in a meager $700 a month.[2] This is what citizens' tax-payer dollars fund in an area of New Mexico heavily burdened by poverty, drugs, poor education, and inadequate health care. And Alcalde's wouldn't be New Mexico's final tribute to Don Juan de Oñate.

In 2005 a second bronze was placed outside Albuquerque's Museum of Art. Again, the city's proposal to honor the conquistador did not meet with unanimous approval: outraged citizens, local artists, and Indians from Acoma Pueblo—the site of Oñate's most onerous atrocities—brought the man's criminal history to the attention of the mayor, city council members, and others. Public discussions were held. Newspaper articles and radio programs attempted to disseminate historical information about the events of 1598-99, as well as about the largely ignored 1680 Pueblo Revolt, which the Indians felt more deserving of a public monument.[3]

But once again, as if there were no one else in our Spanish, Mexican, or New Mexican heritage whose life is more worthy of tribute, those insisting on honoring Oñate had their way. Despite considerable protest, Albuquerque's Hispanic community, or its most reactionary sector, prevailed.[4] Another statue of Oñate would remind us of abuse and annihilation, rubbing raw the trauma Indian peoples of the area have carried for generations.

If you ask around in Mexico, it's difficult to find someone who knows who Don Juan de Oñate was. In Spain he is but a minor footnote in the history of the conquest. It seems that only here in New Mexico, where he committed his greatest crimes, statues are commissioned in his honor. The Albuquerque monument was erected at a cost of $700,000 and occupies a prominent place in front of the city's Museum of Art.

Why not have placed this statue, if it had to be erected, at the multimillion-dollar Hispanic Cultural Center on the city's south side? There, at least, it could be appreciated by the small but influential Hispanic community that wanted it, and by the greater Hispanic community that finally did so little to try to protect the sensibilities of the descendants of those Native Americans who suffered genocide at the hands of the conquistador.

The most the Hispanic community and city of Albuquerque were willing to do—an entirely inadequate concession to so much pain—was to change the monument's name to *La entrada* ("The Entrance"). This "solution" honors the conquistador without explicitly naming him. As a compromise it reflects the failure to assume responsibility that characterizes most such travesties.

But even this would not be the final chapter in our modern-day southwestern homage to Oñate. In the midst of tremendous controversy, a third monument, this one the largest bronze equestrian statue in the world, was erected in El Paso, Texas, in 2007. Honoring violent men crossing borders motivated by the insatiable need to conquer and possess, it is twenty-eight times life-size.

As a symbol, this monument is as tragically coherent with the times we are living as it is offensive to the feelings of those who care. Promoted as a tribute to the border, the project obtained public as well as private funding. Prior to its erection, El Paso's city council was the site of heated discussion; and when one outspoken councilman, Anthony Cobos, spoke out against the statue, he was forced from his job by powerful pro-Oñate interests.

Ignoring the carnage committed so many centuries before, sculptor John Houser and his supporters described Oñate and his band as having brought civilization to New Mexico. In their biased reading of history, the Indians were savages, waiting to be civilized and saved. These people actually speak of the conquest in positive terms.

John Valadéz's 2008 PBS film, *The Last Conquistador*, promised to tell the Indian as well as the Hispanic side of the story—regarding the struggle provoked by the erection of the statue and also the history it depicts. Under the illusion that they would get to tell their side, people at Acoma Pueblo agreed to cooperate with the filmmaker. He included them, but secondarily. At best, the film comes off as a weak pretense at fairness. When it comes to murderers and their victims, there really is no such thing as a level playing field. Simply presenting the opposing points of view hardly translates as fair.

As I worked on this essay, I heard the following tale. Someone reported having seen the legs and torso of Hauser's huge casting on the outskirts of Albuquerque, at the Sandia Pueblo gas station at I-25 and Tramway. She spoke with the driver of the large rig. He told her he was driving the immense pieces south to El Paso, from Wyoming where they had been forged, and his truck had broken down. Ironic that this rendition of Oñate was left stranded at precisely the point along the route that is closest to Acoma.

This story reminds me of another. In Mexico, during the 1960s, an immense stone statue of Tlaloc, the Aztec god of rain, was being transported from its original site in the state of Veracruz to stand before the capital city's new Museum of Anthropology and History. Many felt it was being stolen from its birthplace. As the eighteen-wheeler carrying the transplant passed through the Zócalo—a major scene of the Spaniards' abuse of native peoples—a clear sky suddenly unleashed torrential rain. We who lined the streets to welcome the majestic entity that day knew the rain god had spoken.

In El Paso protest also erupted. And once again those intent upon erecting the statue believed a simple name change would solve the problem. Rather than expressly honoring Oñate, this monstrous monument is now called *The Equestrian*. Don Juan de Oñate was a war criminal: no more, no less. Erecting statues in his honor is like immortalizing Custer, Hitler, Trujillo, Batista, Somoza, Pinochet, Savimbi, Milosevic, Osama bin Laden, or Dick Cheney.

Indian people in New Mexico have a rich history of resistance. One example is the Pueblo Revolt of 1680, a heroic event and one that rarely receives its due. If taught at all in our schools, it is dispatched with a paragraph or two, more often than not inaccurate. I went to elementary, middle, and high school in New Mexico. I remember a quickly glossed-over lesson and no discussion—certainly none from the Indian point of view.

Oñate supporters, not surprisingly many of whom refer to the events of 1680 as excessively bloody, don't even want to hear about the revolt. They judge it too violent and use the argument that always seems to be dredged up in such discussions: why not forget about the past and move forward together?

The Pueblo Revolt took place at the end of the seventeenth century, at what is now San Juan Pueblo. A medicine man by the name of Popé was publicly whipped for practicing his religion. Humiliated, he swore revenge and vowed to drive the Spanish from Indian lands. Popé was a powerful indigenous leader. Despite the many different languages spoken by the peoples of the Rio Grande valley, he was able to unite Keres, Tewa, Tiwa, Towa, Diné, Apache, Ute, and Comanche. Such unity had never been achieved prior to that moment, nor has it been possible since.

More than simply a revolt, this was a revolution launched against what was then the most powerful nation in the world. The Indians succeeded in driving the Spaniards from their lands, all the way back to Mexico City; and for twelve years they remained free of occupation. Following their victory, they are said to have bathed in the rivers to purge themselves of forced baptism in the Catholic faith.

But with an enemy possessing such superior weaponry, freedom couldn't last. In 1692 De Vargas came back into New Mexico intent upon reclaiming what the Indians had taken back. Today the state of New Mexico celebrates De Vargas's campaign in its annual Fiesta of Santa Fe. Modern-day New Mexican apologists say they are commemorating the bloodless re-conquest of the territory. Needless to say, it wasn't bloodless at all. History written by the victor always tends to describe its sieges as bloodless while portraying those who fight for their land and way of life as blood-thirsty savages.

What happened in 1680 was that the violence and oppression of the Spanish occupation had become unbearable and led the people to expel their invaders. Theirs was an act of self-defense, one that not only allowed the Indians to survive but is a primary reason their cultures remain intact today. The Pueblo Revolt, like the nation's early campaigns against the English or the courageous Underground Railroad preceding the Civil War, belongs to all of us. We should all know the history. We should all be proud.

In New Mexico there is no public tribute to the Pueblo Revolt, and no monument to Popé. Several years back such a statue was proposed but was rejected because, it was argued, it would have exalted violence. Yet these same decision makers have no problem erecting monuments to Oñate; his violence, in their eyes, either is exaggerated or must have been justified.[5]

By any reasonable standard—whether one is Acoma, from one of the other Pueblo tribes, Navajo, Apache, Hopi, Hispanic, Mexican, Latino, Chicano, of African, Asian or European American or any other origin, honoring Oñate should provoke disgust. He was no hero, even by the standards of his own time. He came, occupied, converted, pillaged, raped, mutilated, and murdered.

History holds many and varied tales of invasion, occupation, and conquest. None are pretty. But few rival what was perpetrated against the indigenous peoples of the Americas. Acoma stands out as a particularly ugly chapter. It is a tale of treachery, abuse, and extreme violence—spiritual as well as physical. In short: genocide. Between 1591 and 1638 two-thirds of the indigenous population of North America were murdered or perished through the loss of their integrity, a peaceful life, or the diseases intentionally spread by the invaders—foreshadowing today's biological warfare.

Rather than honor one of the leading perpetrators of that genocide, why not initiate healing between descendants of the abusers and the abused? Reconciliation can never work on an uneven playing field. It must begin with a gesture of acknowledgment: the descendants of the perpetrators offering some sign of respect to the descendants of the victims. Removing an Oñate statue, moving it to a less conspicuous place, or funding a monument that memorializes the Indian resistance: any of these might serve as an initial gesture of goodwill. Once some measure of respect is established, both sides of this dispute could come together to listen to one another.

Multiple indigenous and Spanish heritages are rich in our midst; history has even witnessed moments of genuine cooperation. But terrorism perpetrated by the invaders against the invaded is well documented. Healing will only begin when those who inherit the burden of aggression can begin to be sensitive to those whose ancestors lost their right feet at the hands of murderers and thugs.

CAN POETRY MATTER?

for Susan Sherman

All poets and readers of poetry ask the question: can poetry matter? We may pose this question in different ways. We may ask if poetry can matter in the wider world, if it has the power to change or even impact how we think or feel, what we believe, how we act, what we want for ourselves and others. Will it win my lover's heart? Keep my children safe? Can it reverse climate change, feed the hungry, effectively support justice or reverse injustices, end war? Can poetry bring about lasting peace?

The question is not whether an individual poem or series of poems has been important to people throughout history. They have been, and powerfully. Such diverse poets as Sappho, Basho, Nguyen Du,[1] Mevlana Rumi, César Vallejo, Pablo Neruda, Nazim Hikmet, Rilke, Ho Chi Minh, Walt Whitman, Czeslaw

Milosz, Allen Ginsberg, Adrienne Rich, June Jordan, Juan Gelman, and Joy Harjo are only a few of those whose work continues to change lives. The question is, can poetry as process and product—as genre—matter? And if so, how?

We may ask more intimate questions about poetry, less ambitious perhaps but clearly meaningful for our human community. For example: can poetry nurture hope, can it make us aware, teach, comfort us in times of grief, heal, inspire? What is poetry's responsibility to language? Can it reveal mysteries, solve problems? Can it shock us to awareness and action, help us negotiate or persuade? What about oral tradition, everyday conversation, music, accent, inflection, color, risk? How does poetry enrich culture, help write history, retrieve or preserve memory, provide vision and perspective? In what ways does it supplement or perhaps even replace the lies that come down to us in history books written by the victors, biography, essays, even the most thoughtful journalism?

Poetry mattered to my friend Cary Herz. Just a couple of weeks before her death from ovarian cancer, she sent a goodbye e-mail to her friends. She ended her message with a Mary Oliver poem, her parting gift. The poem was "In Blackwater Woods."[2] The gift allowed us to breathe when we received it, and lifted us in recognition when the rabbi read it at Cary's graveside. That poem continues to remind us of our friend, her gentle sensibility, meaningful photography, fierce resistance, and gracious farewell. But it does much more than that. The lessons it holds move on a number of levels. I can think of many such instances when a particular poem or group of poems tempered sorrow, imbued me with courage, flashed an unexpected image, or simply expressed an idea or emotion as nothing else could.

Poems have been smuggled out of prisons, shared on battlefields, passed from hand to hand and generation to generation as they were scratched on walls, written in diaries and recipe books, distributed on street corners, and carried cross-county by hobos riding the freight trains of the 1930s. They have inhabited public spaces and been whispered in ears, bringing otherwise indescribable events and people to life in stunning ways. Their humor makes us laugh. Their truth can take our breath away. Their concise complexity may transmit more, and more powerfully, than any piece of prose. Their ability to evoke emotion often makes them purveyors of experience in ways that more expository writing cannot.

It is obvious that poetry changes language. Cultural change influences what is permissible, what may be judged redundant or acceptable. What startles or reinvents in a poem today, will tomorrow nestle securely in the lexicon. It is also clear that each new communicative tool—the telegraph, telephone, computer, cell phone, iPod, Blackberry, Kindle, and other constantly evolving electronic devices—can rejuvenate poetry. Chatting, twittering, and text-messaging push language toward brevity; urge us to say what we mean, and now. But they also do more. Typographical layout and rhythm emerge from how life is lived. We continue to marvel at old parchments and the beauty of hand-set type, but these rapidly evolving techniques continually reinvent themselves and change how we speak to one another. The way a poet reads out loud to an audience, and that audience's response, can also change a poem forever. Meaning follows.

Perhaps it is poetry's ability to reduce an idea or emotion to its minimum expression that gives it such staying power.

I came to poetry in a particular time and series of places. Like so many in my generation, in school I was forced to commit to memory monotonous poems I did not understand and to which I couldn't relate. One teacher's singsong recitation of Henry Wadsworth Longfellow's "Evangeline" and "Hiawatha" robbed them of interest and meaning. Another's rendition of Edgar Allen Poe's "The Raven" obliterated any connection I might have made between that poem and my own experience. Even Shakespeare's sonnets were rendered boring or unintelligible. This distortion—sadly all too common in what passes for education—convinced me I hated poetry back then.

The first time I felt a poem radically change me was a few years later, just after I'd fled my only year of university. It was 1956. At a party in Albuquerque's East Mountains someone read out loud from a recently published book: City Lights' little black-and-white edition of Allen Ginsberg's *Howl*. I was riveted, not only by the words and cadence but by the ferocity and spirit of its title poem, what it revealed to me about my generation's passion and longing against a backdrop of 1950s conformity, hypocrisy, ugliness, and lies. What it revealed to me about myself.

I wrote to Ginsberg, care of City Lights. I told him I would meet him on a particular street corner in San Francisco, on such and such a date. I remember driving all day and all night, never doubting he would be there. At the appointed time I went to the street corner and waited. Ginsberg didn't show. Years later, when we became friends on New York City's Lower East Side, we laughed at my provincial naïveté.

I was never really part of the Beat scene. My own incipient verse owed more to the traditions of Black Mountain and Deep Image, to William Carlos Williams, and—when I began to live in a Spanish-speaking world—César Vallejo. But "Howl" ripped me open, exposed me to myself, which I believe is one of the things a successful poem must do.

In 1961 I went to Mexico City, the beginning of a quarter-century journey that would include Cuba, North Vietnam, Peru, and Nicaragua. Alone in the new city, I found my way to the Zona Rosa,[3] to the apartment of the U.S. American Beat poet Philip Lamantia and Lucille, the woman who was then his wife. On any given night a group of young poets gathered there—from Mexico, other parts of Latin America, and the United States. Despite the fact that few of us read or spoke the others' language with anything resembling fluency, we shared new poems, listened to unfamiliar rhythms, commented on unexpected subject matter. These impromptu salons pointed up a deep need for a forum in which we might publish, translate, and come to know each other's work.

The Mexican poet Sergio Mondragón and I decided to create such a forum. This was the energized sixties, in one of the most culturally alive urban centers on the continent. We founded and coedited a bilingual literary journal, *El Corno Emplumado / The Plumed Horn*,[4] where we were soon publishing an eclectic mix of work by independent poets from all over the world, including Ginsberg for the first time in Spanish and Ernesto Cardenal for the first in English. The journal ran for eight and a half years. We produced quarterly issues averaging two to three hundred pages. *El Corno Emplumado* was a focal point in a renaissance that lifted cutting-edge literature out of the academy and placed it at the center of creativity and change.

Reading and listening to a great deal of poetry in Spanish also gave me something important. I believe that knowing more than one language greatly enriches one's ability to explore each. If I had learned more than two languages, my relationship to language itself would have benefited even more. Those eight years, in which editing a bilingual journal put me in touch not only with poets writing in English and Spanish but with translations from other languages, provided an intimacy with the written and spoken word that is impossible to overstate.

Physically, in that era before the Internet, writing and publishing depended on inadequate postal systems, the linotype and letterpress capabilities of small one-person print shops, very occasionally a long-distance telephone call. We prided ourselves on our independence. Every day we would visit our neighborhood post office box, where dozens of letters and manuscripts awaited. We walked the streets for advertising, hawked copies of each issue at local bookstores, and sat on our living room floor to fill five- or ten-copy orders destined for everywhere.

This was long before computers, which would later change my own poetry dramatically; or e-mail, which today makes communication with remote parts of the world instantaneous. Cut and paste may be the late twentieth century's greatest gift to poets. Internet research tools and spell-check are equally valuable.

In 1961, coming as I did from a country still repressed by McCarthy's chill, contact with young Latin Americans taught me that poets can write about anything. I'd absorbed the stultifying 1950s notion that politics could not be part of poetry: good poetry, the academy warned, had to be "beyond politics." In Latin America and other parts of the world, poets understood that only imitation, sentimentality, cliché, untruth, or a lack of respect for the word could be dangerous to the poem. We wrote about what we knew, what was most vital to our experience. What was most vital to the experience of many young poets in the 1960s, '70s, and '80s was the need for social change.

In Latin America I also discovered oral tradition. It exists all over the world, of course, including and richly in my own United

States. But, perhaps because their oral traditions were more valued culturally, the poets I met in the 1960s were closer to those traditions than I was to mine. They explored their people's rhythms of speech and included them in their work. When I began doing oral history, especially with women, I too came to understand how vital local jargon, cadence, and inflection can be to the transmission of living ideas; and I began to incorporate ordinary people's speech patterns into my verse. Back in the late 1950s, when I first showed up in New York City as an incipient poet, the novelist and dramatist Paddy Chayefsky had urged me to spend an hour or so a day on a busy city street corner, then come home and see how much of what I'd heard I could accurately record. By the time I got to Latin America I'd developed a practiced ear.

And yes, we believed poetry could change the world. We said as much in a number of the journal's editorials; and the poems we published—by Catholic priests, leftist guerrillas, indigenous shamans, students, literary scholars, and ordinary working men and women—echoed the idea in one way or another. As I say, we were young and naïve and endowed rather more with energy and excitement than with a realistic perception of the relative importance of our own work in the grand scheme of things. We intuited the ways in which the word incarnates and moves—something a number of cultural traditions have known and practiced for millennia.

The best poems inhabit a magical sphere where the word transmutes to energy and energy regroups in ways we do not completely understand. This mystery itself is part of the poem's magic, what gives it its power. Language, sound, silences are—in addition to meaning—made up of molecules, synapse, memory, music, pulse, color, light. Combining these elements in new and different ways traces new and different pathways to and from the poem.

I no longer believe that poetry alone can change the world. But poetry matters, perhaps more than we know. In fact, we ignore or write off its unquantifiable, intuitive, magical qualities at our peril—especially in times of crisis. I am sure poetry has a role to play within the living, vibrant, ever-changing community of those of us who hope we will not perish through our own ignorance, apathy, and greed.

I would like to conclude by reading two poems. The first is mine; it can be considered a political poem, I suppose, but I prefer to think of it as poetic response to all that surrounds us now—the body of the land as well as the body politic. It is, in fact, called "Imagine a Body."[5]

Imagine a Body

I say it is fear. Long way down
from this rocky ledge,
imagine a body
hurtling through air
its years shrinking to seconds
view of the world cut clean,
never, or never again.

I say it is hunger gnawing
at bellies and bones
simple arithmetic
between the teeth
who decides
who deserves to eat
and who to die.

I say what happens to them
can happen to us, you, me,
change of direction
no severance pay
or clean sheets
water salving
lips peeled horizon-dry.

I say denial, self-satisfied
suits, dash of color
the expensive tie.
I say greed
speaking to greed
pointing recognition's finger,
thank you and good day.

In an almost perfect world
they would have to answer
for their crimes.
In the world we have
we are grateful
for comforting discourse
hiding more of the same.

The second is by the great César Vallejo, still not as well-known
as he should be among U.S. American writers and readers. Vallejo
was born in 1892 in a small town in the Peruvian highlands. As
a young man he was a teacher, and produced a couple of early
poetry collections before moving to Paris late in the decade
of the 1920s. He would never return to his native land, but his
astonishing linguistic innovation would change the Spanish
language forever. I think it is safe to say there isn't a poet of note
writing in Spanish who does not owe something to Vallejo.

In the 1930s Vallejo visited a young Soviet Union, prompting several important essays. His greatest book of poetry was published posthumously as *Poemas humanos* (*Human Poems*). He traveled to Spain during that country's civil war, an experience that gave birth to his final book: *Spain, Take from Me This Chalice* (1937). César Vallejo died in Paris in 1938 as he himself predicted in "Black Stone on White Stone," one of the poems in his earlier *Nómina de huesos* (*Litany of Bones*), which begins: "I will die in Paris in a sudden rain, / a day I can already remember." The Vallejo poem I want to end with is called "Masses." Because none of the published translations satisfy me, I will read my own[6]:

Masses

The battle was over,
the combatant dead, and a man approached
pleading: "Don't die, I love you so!"
But the corpse, ay, it kept on dying.

Two came and they too implored:
"Don't leave us! Courage! Return to life!"
But the corpse, ay, it kept on dying.

Twenty, a hundred, a thousand, five hundred thousand
arrived, crying out: "So much love powerless against death!"
But the corpse, ay, it kept on dying.

Millions surrounded him
with a single plea: "Don't leave us, brother!"
But the corpse, ay, it kept on dying.

Then all the earth's inhabitants
surrounded him; the corpse looked at them in sorrow,
  was moved, slowly rose
to embrace the first man; began to walk . . .

So yes, I say, poetry does matter. If we learn to listen, it can
tell us everything.

Words for
El Corno Emplumado

Forty years ago, *El Corno Emplumado* was an independent bilingual poetry journal publishing out of Mexico City. We who were its founders and editors didn't realize it at the time, but over the next couple of years it would enter its definitive crisis, ceding to the unequal forces of government repression and personal trauma. Having survived longer than the vast majority of independent literary ventures of the times, the journal that nurtured difference and advocated for harmony among peoples would succumb, reinventing itself only in memory and inspiration for future generations of poets and artists.

Yet *El Corno Emplumado*—its essence, its meaning—never really died. Like all true weavings of creative expression, its gifts simply took other forms, inhabited new spaces and dimensions.

Copies of its thirty-two issues continue to pass from hand to hand, in Peru, Nicaragua, Mexico, Japan, India, and even in such countries as Bulgaria and South Africa. Four decades after its demise I continue to receive letters from people all over the world who, in their youth, were turned on to poetry and moved to their own diverse forms of creative expression by the magazine. In 1984, recently returned from my almost quarter century in Latin America, I happened to be walking along Fourth Avenue here in New York City one day and passed the Strand, treasure trove of used books. On a high shelf, near the ceiling, I spied one complete set of the magazine. The price tag was $3,500!

The cultural pendulum swings back and forth, following the movement of the political pendulum that registers periods of creative silencing or renewal. After we were forced to stop publishing, I migrated from Mexico to Cuba, Cuba to Nicaragua, and finally back to the United States. Although I lost much along the way—for example, Nicaragua's Corinto port was mined just as I prepared to send my belongings by sea, forcing me to reduce them to their minimum expression when faced with the only alternative of sending them by air—I managed to hold on to one complete set of *El Corno*. It continues to sit, weathered but proud, on my bookshelf.

Every once in a while, usually because I am asked to write about the journal or give an interview about those times, I find myself turning its pages, marveling at our youthful energy, audacity, eye for cutting-edge work or tolerance for work that was not so good. I cringe at the paucity of work by good women poets. I am occasionally embarrassed by some inclusion that is frankly bad. But I am also, and most often, freshly excited by the important project Sergio Mondragón and I managed to birth and sustain through the 1960s.

A few years ago when Anne Mette Nielsen and Nicolenka Beltrán approached me about making a film of this history, the first thing I noticed was that they were roughly the ages we were when we embarked upon our adventure, that is to say, in their mid-twenties. Their enthusiasm was obvious. And several years later, when the film premiered, their brilliance and creative powers were as well. I was fortunate to be able to attend one of the Mexican premieres, in the context of the Guadalajara Book Fair some three years back. The viewing room, packed with young poets, attested to *El Corno*'s continued relevance.

I want to honor our tenacity and resilience at a time when U.S. poetry was just beginning to emerge from the long chill of McCarthyism and Latin American poetry was being bloodied by dictatorships and hidden or dispersed in the recesses of a people's resistance. I honor the enormous web of hearts and voices we brought together in the journal's pages, our independence and our love. I honor Sergio Mondragón and Robert Cohen, the first cofounder and coeditor for most of *El Corno*'s life, the second for editing the journal with me during its last year. It is a great pleasure for me to share this panel with Jerome Rothenberg and Cecilia Vicuña, co-panelists whose work appeared in the magazine, and to recognize Susan Sherman, who also published with us back then and is here tonight.

Age brings us all to a place where death visits our living and claims fellow poets and creative co-conspirators. For this reason I would also like to pronounce the names of some of the wonderful poets and artists whose work appeared in *El Corno* and who are no longer with us. I do this not to bring gloom upon this gathering, but rather to remember their creative input. By speaking their names I hope to bring them into this circle, welcome them to memory. The list does not pretend to be complete, only representative. Please join me in remembering Bella Akhmadulina, Rafael Alberti, Daisy Aldan, M. S. Arnoni, Antón Arrufat, Dubjinski Barefoot, José Bartolí, Agustí Bartra, José Carlos Becerra, Arnold Belkin, Washington Benavides, Mario Benedetti, Carol Bergé, Paul Blackburn, Ray Bremser, Besmilr Brigham, Charles Bukowski, Rosario Castellanos, Otto-René Castillo, Aimé Césaire, Carlos Coffeen Serpas, Bruce Conner, Cid Corman, Julio Cortázar, Elise Cowen, Robert Creeley, Pablo Antonio Cuadra, Salvador Dali, Roque Dalton, Rubén Darío, Ned Davison, Fielding Dawson, Giorgio De Chirico, Elaine de Kooning, Eliseo Diego, Ed Dorn, Manuel Durán, Larry Eigner, T. S. Eliot, León Felipe, Waldo Frank, A. Frederic Franklin, Buckminster Fuller, Rabbi Everett Gendler, Allen and Louis Ginsberg, Jacobo Glantz, Mathias Goeritz, Otto-Raul González, Saul Gottlieb, Nicolás Guillén, Judith Gutiérrez, Marguerite Harris, Javier Heraud, Herman Hesse, Spencer Holst, Efraín Huerta, Fayad Jamís, Lenore Kendal, Paul Klee, Franz Kline, Seymour Krim, Philip Lamantia, Red Lane, Denise Levertov, d. a. levy, José Lezama Lima, Enrique Lihn, Walter Lowenfels, Jackson MacLow, Ana Mairena, Mariano, Juan Martínez, Thomas Merton, Ernesto Mejía Sánchez, Henry Miller, Eugenio Montale, Beltrán Morales, Harold Norse, Pablo Neruda, Luís Rogelio Nogueras, Heberto Padilla, Kenneth Patchen, Octavio Paz, Carlos Pellicer, Christopher Perret, Francis Picabia, Virgilio Piñera, Ezra Pound, Ann Quin, Milton Resnick, Yanis Ritsos, Vicente Rojo, Henri Rousseau, Juan Rulfo, Jaime Sabines, Laurette Sejourne, Rini Templeton, Edmundo Valadéz, César Vallejo, Rudolfo Walsh, Hannah Weiner, Keith Wilson, William Carlos Williams, and Louis Zukofsky.

I was recently in Mexico City, launching a new book of poetry in Spanish translation. My old and very dear friend, the Mexican poet and cultural promoter Thelma Nava, was one of the presenters. Remembering those years, in which her journal, *Pájaro Cascabel*, and *El Corno* shared the beautiful task of bringing new poets to publication, she said, "In those days there was a great solidarity among all the publishers, something that would be inconceivable today." I fear Thelma is right, but hope she is wrong. I hope that spirit of solidarity lives somewhere; because only when we put the work itself before petty jealousies and competitions can we keep the passion of creativity alive. Individual poems only require the talent of the individual poet. A movement requires shared commitment, excitement, and exchange.

It is that excitement and exchange that remains *El Corno's* most important legacy.

THE LIVING SILENCE OF A
PLACE LIKE KIET SEEL

In pondering my Latin American work—the oral history, the essays, and some of the poetry—the first thing that comes to mind is how different the world in which I worked back then was from the one we inhabit today. Not only geography, but time and expectation have shifted. Then my life and work were cradled in hope; more than simply hope, the absolute conviction that I was part of a movement that was creating a better, more just world.

A pervasive discouragement now characterizes our world. This is not merely the result of those understandings and complexities that come with age. It is a product of these times' appalling restriction of freedoms, narrowing of opportunity; a response to the fact that so much power has been concentrated in the hands of arch criminals—criminals we ourselves put in office or allow to remain there—and that the field of action for those working for positive change has been so drastically reduced.

Our world is more violent, more dangerous, and a future of justice so much less palpable than it was when the Civil Rights Movement achieved its initial goals, U.S. citizens helped stop the American war of aggression in Vietnam, the Second Wave of Feminism was at the height of its power and influence, and I lived and worked in revolutionary Cuba or Sandinista Nicaragua.

We are faced with an interesting dichotomy. On the one hand some of our struggles have borne fruit. Among these are the recognition that we must address climate change and global warming, the increased expectations and possibilities for women's lives, more acceptance of and respect for peoples deemed "different" by mainstream society, important advances in what we know about how to teach and learn, a more in-depth understanding of the mind/body connection, a broader more inclusive vision of history, and a renewed recognition of the vital centrality of stories. On the other, our struggles seem to stagnate beneath the weight of greed, violence, recklessness, and war. Our children's is the first generation that cannot expect to live better than their parents. And our government is devastating the lives of innocent people throughout the world. I am speaking not only economically, but morally as well.

Class inequities are, if anything, more entrenched than they were thirty or forty years ago. And where they are not, the trend is down rather than up. The gap between the obscenely wealthy and the miserably poor has widened. Race issues have shown themselves to be many-layered and more complex than we once imagined. Fundamentalist extremists within all the major religious configurations have spawned an ignorance and violence that permeate the relationships between men and women, adults and children, powerful nations and those most vulnerable to their designs.

After my return to the United States in 1984, retrieved memories of incest led me to understand that the invasion of a child's body by a perpetrator with power over his victim has everything to do with the invasion of a small nation by one that is stronger and more powerful. An international hegemony of power, in which a single country or system dominates, has produced horrific policies such as that of the preemptive strike. And the cover-ups are ever more blatant. State terrorism has achieved levels unimaginable even a few years back. Vast numbers of people are manipulated through fear. And we are poisoning our nest past the point where we may be able to reclaim it.

Most of my work in Latin American oral history—the books about women's lives, the poetry and essays written between the mid-1960s and late 1980s—was created in an atmosphere of genuine possibility. I believed in the socialist alternative. I lived its promise, first in Cuba and then in Nicaragua. Additionally, feminism gave me the tools with which I began to try to decipher the issue of power.

Mine was the privilege of involvement, of daily participation, of constant discussion and the energy that comes from believing victory is achievable. Even as I began to challenge some of the premises, even when I questioned certain interpretations and/ or the motives of some of those doing the interpreting, what we sought seemed right to me. Not only right but possible. This atmosphere of confidence and hope produced work that was daring, sometimes somewhat one-dimensional but always honest and inspired by that vision of justice that is still, for me, very much an ideal.

Today—older, aware of the complexities of my own history, with many more questions, and inhabiting a different world with a vastly different correlation of forces—I am deeply discouraged. Not depressed, but discouraged. I still believe in the goals for which we struggled throughout the last half of the twentieth century, those for which so many died and for which so many continue to struggle today. I still envision a world in which justice reigns, in which men of obscene greed are no longer permitted to murder and maim at will, in which health, education, art, and the well-being of our planet are cherished rather than trampled or discarded in the name of quick profit.

But the brave experiments aimed at securing such a world have mostly been defeated by forces of such perverse and pervasive criminality that what would have been unacceptable even ten years back is today seen as inevitable or "normal." I am not by nature a depressive person, but I would be out of touch with reality not to feel acute discouragement.

Despite all this, I continue to subscribe to the struggles for peace and justice, the efforts toward economic and racial and gender and cultural equalities, the desperate need to effect a change in U.S. foreign and domestic policies, a turnabout to the rampant contamination of earth, air, water, and what we put into our bodies. I have come to understand incest and the sexual abuse of children as intimately linked to the manipulation and abuse of communities and nations, and continue to imbue my work with this understanding. The silences and lies corrode integrity as much in one scenario as in the other.

Making these connections and others has made my work richer. But the work itself no longer draws on an energy of hope. Today I struggle because it is morally imperative, not because I expect success.

Gathering Rage: The Failure of 20th Century Revolutions to Develop a Feminist Agenda,[1] my 1992 book about the Left's inability to embrace feminist principles, broached issues and realities I could no longer ignore. Many of the ideas in that book were taken further, and validated, by the women who told me their stories in *Sandino's Daughters Revisited: Feminism in Nicaragua* (1994).[2] When the latter was translated into Spanish and became available to the women whose stories it included, the book provoked gratitude, profound turmoil, and further exploration.[3]

But the work in which this crisis is most palpable, both in the process of the writing and in the product itself, is *When I Look into the Mirror and See You: Women, Terror, and Resistance.*[4] Although I began the interviews and research in 1996, the book wouldn't see publication until 2003. Several times during those seven years, I doubted I would be able to continue. I felt paralyzed. For a time, finishing seemed utterly beyond my capabilities. The story I knew I must tell was infinitely more complex than those I had grappled with before. I wasn't aware of it at the time, but I was experiencing the culmination of my own personal version of the political/emotional crisis that has affected so many of us over the past two decades.

It wasn't only a changed world that required a different approach. I myself had changed. While my core beliefs remain solid, my understanding of how we may be able to move from point A to point B—or fail to do so—is more nuanced, takes into account a greater range of variables, and seems more difficult at a variety of levels. Because I value process over product, because I deeply believe in sharing the unfinished and imperfect, I managed to readdress the challenge. By the time *When I Look into the Mirror and See You* was published, it had become—for me and for others—an important piece of our ongoing conversation about power, memory, personal and public space, ends, and means.

The story's two protagonists are not the only ones revealed in the mirror of human reflection this book presents; the author is as well. In this book I am more present, more exposed, more vulnerable, and more questioning: left raw by the unspeakable crimes and deeply courageous responses of our times.[5]

And here is where I would like to speak about a strange turn my interests have taken. Of great refuge and inspiration, since I returned to the United States in 1984, have been the ancient ruins and rock art left by those who preceded us upon this land. Living in the southwestern part of the United States, I am surrounded by the remnants of several ancient cultures: the Ancestral Puebloans (sometimes called Anasazi), Fremont and Mogollón, the unnamed nomads who roamed these lands ten thousand years ago, even peoples from further south who interacted and traded with those who inhabited the canyons and cave alcoves of the Colorado Plateau—what we know today as Utah, Arizona, Colorado, and New Mexico.

As in my own life's journey, the border dividing the northern and southern land masses of our continent has been contested, largely irrelevant, malleable, ultimately fictitious. The border exists, with all the aggression of its divisions, unsolved crimes, human and drug trade, murders, law enforcement (both official and unofficial), and pain. Only its meaning is not what it seems.

At first, visits to Chaco, Mesa Verde, Canyon de Chelly, Paquimé, Hovenweep, Wupatki, Betatakin, Bandelier, Pecos, Puyé, and other such sites were pleasure outings, times of relaxation and delight. They remain so. But they have acquired an added dimension and immediacy, a relevance to my life and thought I could not have imagined some years back. If it did not conjure such religious or clichéd connotations, I would be inclined to use the word pilgrimage. I have come home.

It was on a recent hike to the less accessible ruin called Kiet Seel,[6] in the extreme north-central part of Arizona, that I first began to equate the experience of listening for the echoes of long-silent voices to that of seeking out and recording the voices of the women in many of my books on Latin America. Despite centuries of silence, the same interactive give-and-take of openness and reception, observation and voice, listening and recording, interpretation and representation is involved. It is as if it is happening all over again, but the raw material is so much more tenuous, the results less tangible or specific, the lessons embryonic in form. This time around, there is a space that was missing then.

It is a space that would appear to be empty.

It is not.

And here I will digress for a moment to tell a story I hope may clarify my approach to this sort of space, its hidden secrets, and the meaning it holds for me. The year 2004 marked the fiftieth anniversary of the death of the Mexican painter Frida Kahlo. I recently returned from Mexico, where commemorations of her life and work abound. One of these struck me as particularly intriguing.

When Frida died, her husband, the great muralist Diego Rivera, locked the bathroom off her bedroom and ordered that no one open it. It is presumed by some that Frida died in that bathroom. Close Rivera family friend Dolores Olmedo became the director of the house where Frida was born and lived with Diego—the blue house in Coyoacán that would become the

Frida Kahlo Museum. Olmedo obeyed Diego's wishes. But this past year she too died, and a new museum director was named. She immediately asked, "What's behind that door?" and when told, directed it be unlocked.

Inside the bathroom were literally hundreds of indigenous *huipiles*, artfully embroidered cotton shifts like the one I am wearing today. The bathtub was filled with them. There were Frida's jewels, her makeup, even her prosthesis (they had had to amputate her leg in the last months of her life, and she briefly wore an artificial one). The writer Elena Poniatowska, in an article for *La Jornada de México*, says there were enough outfits that for six months the artist could have worn a different one each day. The contents of that bathroom are now being cleaned and mended by experts, and are gradually being put on display.

Mexico is enthralled with this revelation. But it is not the contents of that bathroom that most interest me. I am powerfully intrigued by the space itself: off-limits for half a century and now—because of an order given and followed—part of the public domain. As I entered the section of Frida's bedroom to which the public has access, I could see the door to the bathroom standing slightly ajar. I strained to be able to peer through its narrow opening. My eyes traveled to the amorphous shapes visible as splotches of color behind the opaque glass brick that forms the bathroom's corner wall. I glimpsed a row of shapes hanging from what I assumed might be a shower curtain rod.

What does it mean that this space has suddenly been made accessible? Is there such a thing as sacred space? If so, under what circumstances may space be transgressed or transformed, and what can happen when it is? I speak from a secular point

148

of view; perhaps I should use the word *living* rather than *sacred*. Yes, space that is alive.

Is there an energy pattern or some other tangible physical force that indicates to us that the nature of a space has changed? Are the sound waves it emits, the temperature it expels, altered? If so, are all or only some of us privy to these changes? Is the place itself transformed, or is our perception of it different as a result of what happened there and what that means to each of us?

As regards the bathroom in the Blue House in Coyoacán, are we who enter that previously forbidden place and repossess the painter's personal items intruding upon Frida's life, or Diego's? What, besides *huipiles* and a prosthetic leg, lived in that locked room? What did its walls hide, what mysteries did it embrace? What can its being made available mean to us now—or to them then? Is time only linear?

I am fascinated by spaces once used for one purpose being opened to another. In ways I find difficult to articulate, unlocking Frida Kahlo's bathroom bears a profound relevance to the act of stepping into an ancient ruin, a space where people once worked and slept and spoke and cooked and ate and played. There is a similar retrieval of objects that were once everyday utensils of the living and are now legacies from the dead. Have time and changing cultures altered them, and if so how? A similar discourse asks that we contemplate, question, decipher. We are presented with the same sort of *desdoblamiento:* an unfolding, splitting off from or dividing from itself.

I had no training in oral history when I began, in the late 1960s and early 1970s, to interview, research, and write what would become *Cuban Women Now*; *Cuban Women Twenty Years Later*; *Spirit of the People: Vietnamese Women Two Years from the Geneva Accords; El pueblo no sólo es testigo: La historia de Dominga; Sueños y realidades de un guajiricantor; Inside the Nicaraguan Revolution: The Story of Doris Tijerino; Sandino's Daughters; Christians in the Nicaraguan Revolution;* and *Risking a Somersault in the Air,* among other books. I learned through trial and error.

Today, as I stand in the silence of a place like Kiet Seel, listening for the voices of peoples long disappeared, I am acutely aware that I have no formal training in anthropology or archeology. But formal training isn't everything. My life experience has taught me how dangerous it is to impose our twentieth- and twenty-first-century cultural biases on others (anthropologists referring to one of the large anthropomorphic representations on the rock wall in Horseshoe Canyon as "the Holy Ghost figure" comes to mind).

I possess neither the academic training, glossary of terms, physical strength, nor presumption to be an "expert" on these forebears and their lives. Instead, I bring to such sites a poet's tools, a photographer's eye, the particular sensibilities of a mother, grandmother, and woman-identified woman, a reverence for life in all its forms, a healthy skepticism of all the reductionist theory that has kept us from seeing life's overall patterns, and the conviction that justice and equality are not outmoded concepts. Even when I am not thoroughly versed in them, I am familiar with and respectful of the beliefs and feelings of those direct descendants—the Hopi and Pueblo peoples who inherit and in their daily practice refer back to those legacies left in rock—and of the Navajo who are today's caretakers of the ruin.

My root knowledge comes from years of experience with people who have nothing to lose but their oppression. It comes from exploring cultural as well as personal memory; from struggling to divest myself of the Eurocentrism, classism, racism, sexism, and homophobia with which all who come up in a society like ours are burdened from birth; and from an ongoing exploration of power and a passion for the language that describes—as precisely as possible—its uses and abuses. My knowledge comes from learning to touch, listen, see.

A little more than a month ago two friends and I hiked the nine miles into Kiet Seel. We stood among its rooms and surveyed the evidence of a ceramic pot seemingly just about to be refilled with river or rain water, ears of corn as if just a moment ago bitten clean of their kernels, a broken wisp of yucca rope, bits of flint tools, and the perch-poles that only eight hundred years ago hosted brightly feathered macaws traded from neighbors to the south. The stories—the history—entered my pores in much the same way as those I collected from the Cuban and Nicaraguan women whose words I gathered into my books.

My days of listening to women's stories, interpreting those stories, and offering them in book form may be over. Or maybe not. What I know is that my curiosity and need move more often now in another direction: toward cultures that preceded by millennia this era of misplaced power and consumer violence. Stillness and intuition are once more called upon to suggest answers only very partially revealed. Learning to look, wait, and listen again becomes imperative.

Just as there were those a quarter century ago who trivialized my books of oral history because they were not impartial, or because most of them included only women's voices, or because they often veered from whatever academic line happened to be fashionable at the time, there will be those today who will not see a connection between the threats to our survival and a hundred or so people who built and inhabited and then disappeared from a site that astounds us with its stunning mystery. The Kayenta Ancestral Puebloans of Kiet Seel lived in their 160-room alcove a mere fifty years (1230-86). They left sophisticated tools, utensils, and an art that speaks to us of what their lives may have been like. I look up and find a highly stylized and deeply incised petroglyph of a snake on the ruin's back wall. Surprisingly detailed pictographs of turkeys adorn another, their creams and pale greens and browns still vivid after all these years. The images may have been made by shamans, artists, ordinary adults, or children. They may represent that which was familiar or desired. There is no inherited language holding clues to who these people were, no written code to be deciphered, scant road signs by which we may see beyond the landscape that is to the landscape that was, few mechanisms for bridging the distance of time.

How rooms were fitted to rooms and a community shaped by the high alcove that held it speak to me of a knowledge of seasons and taste for need-fulfillment rather than greed.

We cannot read the answers to our questions, but must look for them in wind, soil, human waste, wall paintings, tools, rock, plant and animal life, and in our own imaginations. And for our imaginations to offer up those clues we seek, we must of course have spent time—perhaps a lifetime—exploring the dialectical relationship between reason and intuition, science and creativity, evidence and that which evidence so often obscures.

We can no longer live only in a world of "fact," for fact is ever changing and has today been twisted beyond recognition. Neither can we hide in a world of poetic license, flights of fancy, the intuitive as the only reality there is. To truly inhabit, feel comfortable in, and use that space that appears empty but is not, we must keep on fighting against the current of numbing manipulation and seek the connections those who would keep on heaping death upon this earth hope we will never find.

With gratitude I touch this space in ruins long abandoned, but vibrant with possibility.

BETRAYAL

In Mexico, before Easter, they burn giant papier-mâché effigies of Judas in every village square and city plaza. In the patio of the house where the great artist Frida Kahlo was born and died—the blue house that is a museum to her art and spirit—a dozen ten-foot-tall Judases escaped the flames. They remain as cultural icons, standing guard as if in eternal defiance. Symbolic as they are of the ultimate betrayal, we at first see folk art; then shudder as their mythical representation enters our consciousness. In Christian iconography Judas is the betrayer who takes the rap for all others.

Now it seems the kiss that gave birth to the tradition might not have been the betrayal we've been led to believe. Centuries of political propaganda may have twisted the truth. Scholars have recently stumbled upon an alternate storyline. According to the Gospel of Judas,[1] found on the Egyptian desert seventeen hundred years after it was written, Jesus himself asked the disciple we revile to denounce him to the Roman authorities. The act would lead to crucifixion, necessary to free Jesus' spirit from his body: an old Gnostic belief.

The Gospel of Judas—tattered papyrus pages in a worn leather binding—came to light in the 1970s. Its Coptic characters had been translated from the Greek a century after it was written. The text describes Jesus telling Judas he will "exceed" the other disciples. "For you will sacrifice the man that clothes me," the translation tells us Jesus is reported to have said to his follower. That the gospels of Matthew, Mark, Luke, and John have come down as the "official story," while this text has been hidden for so long, has imbued Judas's life with a very different symbolism. During a series of early Christian councils, powerful political factions hammered out the beliefs that would shape future Church dogma.[2] Think Democratic and Republican conventions.

In the discovery of this narrative the worst becomes the best, the assumed betrayer the most dearly beloved. Judas not only consented to do his master's bidding, but to take upon his shoulders an eternity of vilification and scorn. Had the political power of the day allowed widespread dissemination of this text, had it challenged the easy authority of the more familiar gospels, how many male children throughout the Christian world might today answer to the name Judas?

The traditional reading of Judas's act was never only about a follower turning his mentor in, for his own gain or at his teacher's request. It became symbolic as well of centuries of anti-Semitism. Popular images of the disciple come down to us with bug eyes and bulbous nose: the stereotypical Jew-hating features. This kiss bears a many-layered and racist iconography.[3]

More important, the discovery in recent decades of a number of alternative Christian texts—the Dead Sea Scrolls and the Gospel of Mary Magdalene, to name only two—gives rise to a much more interesting discussion about betrayal. What is the unchallengeable word of God for some is an impediment to rational thought for others. If there are many storylines, which one of them—if any—is true? The fundamentalist's Divine Word may not be so divine after all. I don't believe betrayal of religious dogma to be such a bad thing.

Betrayal. How does it move among us? To what historical distortions does it give birth, what crimes does it justify? And what does it mean? What whole group of people may be attacked for centuries, their abusers encouraged as some ancient twist of hatred is allowed to fester and grow? To whose advantage does the bit of political propaganda-cum-dogma accrue? Who loses? What moral standard, sense of community, or praise song to life is bolstered or breached? Clearly there are differences of interpretation, dependent upon time, place, allegiance, and point of view. Deeply personal betrayals almost always have larger implications. Mass betrayals shape individual lives in unexpected and often devastating ways.

The rules may be made by an evil cabal or spring courageous from a profound moral sensibility. Germany's Third Reich betrayed its Jewish citizens, who were, after all, also Germans. Thousands of non-Jewish rescuers risked their own lives protecting and ultimately saving many of their Jewish neighbors. This brave resistance defied laws that had been imposed precisely in order to rid the country of its Jewish citizens. It betrayed secular policy in obedience to a higher ethical calling, the belief that all humans deserve life and well-being. Today few would question which act was betrayal.

There are also the intimate betrayals.

Consider the grandfather who fondles his granddaughter. She trusts him, but decades later will remember only the piercing glint in his eyes, those carefully manicured fingernails. The pedophile priest who lures his altar boys to shadowy sacristy rooms: divine morality, hierarchical authority, and innocent trust—all betrayed. The rabbi who, for years and beneath a modest lap robe, molests his terrified preteen Torah student; while in an adjacent kitchen the student's mother prepares their weekly milk and cookies. The teacher who sells a grade for sexual favors. The coach whose locker-room conduct never makes it into the local paper, its sports coverage focused as it is on home team pride.

For betrayals to exist there must first of all be trust. We are not betrayed by our enemies but by our friends: parents, mentors, lovers, respected public officials, or benevolent authority figures. I must add to my list the revolutionary leader who for almost two decades abused his step-daughter, convincing her that it was her political duty to satisfy his perverse needs. He was her father, the leader of the political organization to which she also belonged, and the president of her country. A stunning example of the powerful taking criminal advantage of the powerless.[4]

Consider the husband who hides his affairs with other women—is it betrayal only when secrecy is involved?—or the wife who goes with other men. Do ideas about gender dismiss one while punishing the other? How does social convention punish or forgive betrayal? Is the act itself or a successful cover-up of the act more injurious?

Consider the boy or man who uses and abuses available

friendship. The teenage girl who jilts a best friend, seeking status with more popular girls. Men and women who grow up learning to take advantage in school or church or business or society. The team that secures a crooked win. The president who betrays a nation.

Remember all those Native Americans who drove their pickups across miles of badlands to cast their ballots in the presidential election of 2000, only to be told they lacked the requisite number of picture IDs? Or the largely black would-be voters in a Louisiana parish who got the recorded message on their phones: "Don't worry if you couldn't make it to the polls today; you can always go back tomorrow"? Then there were the hundreds of thousands, perhaps even millions, who did vote but whose votes were never counted. Our suspect electoral machine, hiding behind the catch-all phrase "democracy in action," betrayed its citizens in 2000 and again in 2004. And it took each individual betrayal to weave the collective betrayal that for eight long years had us—and so much of the world—in its grip.

The newly uncovered explanation of Judas's actions also reminds me of those news stories one stumbles upon from time to time, in which a hurting misfit, often presumed to be armed, taunts the police until one of them shoots him dead. We realize that the man, despairing and desperate, had wanted to end his life. Lacking the courage or ability to pull the trigger himself, he created a situation in which someone would pull it for him. Why couldn't Jesus of Nazareth have turned himself in to the Roman authority? Today's sad figures appear only briefly on our nightly news and are then forgotten. Unlike Judas, they respond to no higher directive, occupy no iconic place in history.

Perhaps my generation's most exhaustively analyzed betrayal was the one leading to Ernesto Che Guevara's 1967 capture and murder in a remote area of the Bolivian mountains. The Old Woman with the Goats. We know her from hearsay, from a brief diary entry: directions asked for and given, and the foreboding that she would offer information for a paltry sum. Which, it seems, she did.

But whose was the bedrock betrayal here: Cuba, which sent an idealistic band of men and women into a culture they didn't know? The Bolivian Communist Party, which, unable to control the *guerrilla*, abandoned it? The CIA, whose betrayal of a continent is filled with so many lesser, contributing, betrayals? Or that threadbare and hungry woman who earned a few pesos for informing on a cause she couldn't have understood? The greater the historical distance, the more angles from which an event may be judged.

In El Salvador, in 1975, a revolutionary poet named Roque Dalton was murdered by members of his own organization. Strategic differences, opportunism, jealousy, and fear spread lies, then led to the unthinkable. Years later, the martyred poet's son interviewed the man responsible for his father's death. The son looked the murderer—long-since tarnished in stature—in the eyes. He did not flinch. He wanted to know why. The murderer was sorry; the act had been the greatest mistake of his life, he said. Betrayal was not avenged—impossible to avenge such an act—but life for that son became, perhaps, a little easier.

In the United States in the early 1950s, at the beginning of the Cold War period, a New York working-class couple named Julius and Ethel Rosenberg were accused of conspiracy to commit espionage, "to give the secret of the atom bomb to the Soviets," the enemy that just a few years earlier had been our World War II ally in the fight against fascism. Now the United States was at war in Korea. In an era of anti-communist hysteria,

160

the Rosenbergs were arrested, tried, and sentenced to die in the electric chair. Every scientist with knowledge of atomic fusion insisted the simple drawing placed in evidence could not possibly enable anyone to fabricate the bomb. None of these scientists were called to testify.

Julius and Ethel maintained their innocence. A worldwide movement surged against the executions. Two little boys would be orphaned. Yet the machinery of narrow nationalism and the perverse need to scapegoat someone could not be stopped. On July 19, 1953, minutes before the Jewish Sabbath, the couple was put to death. A state, gone mad with anti-communist fanaticism, had betrayed two of its citizens and millions more. It wasn't the first time, nor would it be the last.

Family betrayal, as well, played a significant role in this story. Ethel Rosenberg's brother, David Greenglass, and his wife, Ruth, were also arrested and charged. But they were given the option of turning state's evidence. If they supported the government's accusation, if they implicated Julius and Ethel, they were told, their lives would be spared. No death in the electric chair for them. No cruel separation from their own two children for Ruth, and a relatively short prison sentence for David. And so brother betrayed sister, mother betrayed daughter, and the crime was consummated.⁵

Michael was ten when his parents were murdered, Robert, six. Thanks to a loving and supportive community, they survived further state repression, were adopted by people who helped them begin to heal, and are today proud of their parents' legacy. Their children are proud. Their grandchildren will be proud.

The Greenglasses, on the other hand, dressed their betrayal in secrecy. It became the family secret, never to be divulged. When David came out of prison, the couple changed their surname. Silence was cast upon their children and grandchildren, who kept or never knew the terrible history. Betrayal became the wall that separated sisters and brothers, cousins, and other relatives. But the final chapter in this tale of two families has not been written. There may yet be another unfolding, a brave new energy capable of breaking through secrecy's destructive wall. In 2002 David Greenglass publicly admitted that he had lied under oath about having observed his sister typing her husband's notes.[6]

Ethel and Julius Rosenberg were not accused of having committed treason, but of conspiracy to commit treason. None of the evidence presented proved even the lesser charge. Nevertheless, the word treason screamed across the front pages of newspapers and rang loud from the mouths of radio and TV newscasters. Because of the way in which the Rosenberg case was depicted in the corporate media, and because our history books make little and deceptive mention of the events leading up to and surrounding the trial or executions, few today have anything beyond the fabricated discourse. The case has become synonymous with treason—in political terms the greatest betrayal—and the Rosenbergs, at least in the mainstream mind, have been indelibly labeled as traitors.

Is the idea of betrayal or treason enough to change the course of history? Can a person become a traitor not because of what he or she did, but because of what he or she is perceived to have done? The perfect traitor, like the perfect storm, must often only satisfy the requirements of time and place: a government's need of a scapegoat or a people's fabricated lust for revenge. The Rosenbergs' sons, Michael and Robert Meeropol, have spent years researching and telling the real story of their parents' lives.

It may be interesting to acknowledge the ways in which the march of history changes and how easily society still may invent a Judas figure or scapegoat a couple such as the Rosenbergs by targeting the hated Jew. As anti-racist work progresses, the worn stereotypes begin to topple. We have a very long way to go before we must no longer struggle against racism and anti-Semitism, but we have come to a point when the questions can be posed—and greater numbers of people listen.

Writers often tell the storylines of our ideologies before the population in general is able to acknowledge them. This is the power of literature. Susan Gubar's book, for example, references a Jorge Luis Borges story written in 1944 which suggests that God "stooped to become man for the redemption of the human race," one who would sin and "be condemned to damnation," and that God "chose an abject existence: He was Judas." Borges was a magnificent storyteller but his work was tainted by anti-Semitism.[7]

Treason is most often a political category. In the 1970s a CIA agent named Philip Agee began to question the morality of his work. Like Daniel Ellsberg around the same time, Agee made classified material public. Ellsberg released the Pentagon Papers, which exposed the criminality of U.S. policy in Vietnam.[8] Agee wrote a memoir, which named dozens of CIA undercover agents around the world. Both men were considered traitors by their organizational superiors. Both unquestionably contributed to a revival of reason, and restoration of peace.[9]

Following the horrendous attacks of September 11, 2001, U.S. Americans were devastated, distraught, in mourning. Personal and collective loss weighed heavy on our national psyche. For a few brief moments—days, perhaps weeks—our political leadership might have led us into a collective meditation on the attacks, an honest discussion of Why Us? We might have embarked upon an era of openness and a more nuanced understanding of other peoples, their cultures, and the fanaticism that can overpower them. Wiser leadership would have guided our emotions more thoughtfully. We might have experienced a more nuanced period of grief, heightened our awareness of why such rage is expressed, begun to work toward answers, and known the relief of healing.

Instead, the machinery of betrayal—always at the ready—was put into motion. A foundering administration leapt at the opportunity to consolidate power and push its political agenda. Hundreds of thousands here and around the world would pay the price. Lies were told and repeated, alliances sought and set. The loss of three thousand lives was used to justify the murder of hundreds of thousands—all in the name of national security. We would protect our borders. We would promote democracy. We would police the world.

A number of years later the Zacarias Moussaoui case pushed betrayal in conflicting directions. Moussaoui was believed by U.S. law enforcement to have been the twentieth hijacker, who somehow missed being on one of those planes-turned-weapons on September 11, 2001. He admitted to sharing the criminals' ideals. It is still unclear whether happenstance caused him to miss out on the operation or he was sidelined because of mental instability. As all those who hijacked the planes were dead, he became the scapegoat: the man upon whom a nation's rage could be unleashed. He didn't really do anything, but might have known about the crime to be committed or imagined he could have been part of it—and did not attempt to hide his satisfaction about that crime or his rage against the United States.

Moussaoui's trial evolved into a grim farce. The prosecution brought in a stream of survivors to testify to the horror of the operation, going so far as to play and replay a tape of the last several minutes aboard one of the planes—evidence unrelated to the man on trial. Without any proof that this man had anything at all to do with what was perpetrated that awful day, it had to be enough that he wished he had been involved. The defense, struggling against its client's own self-incriminating outbursts, should have had no trouble proving him mentally ill: incompetent or worse.

This trial moved far beyond any ordinary court of law. It wasn't an act that was on trial, but the accused man's gloating versus the public's perception of responsibility and desire for vengeance. Like the Rosenbergs, Moussaoui was being tried for conspiracy to commit a crime rather than for having committed one. But this is where the similarity ends. The Rosenbergs insisted upon their innocence. Moussaoui tried to take credit for a crime in which, despite fantasy claims, he most probably had no part.

Betrayal was everywhere in evidence in Zacarias Moussaoui's trial. Many U.S. Americans, especially some of those who lost loved ones in the crimes of September 11, felt Moussaoui's conviction might somehow assuage their sense of betrayal by a system incapable of protecting them. Some, however, also including a few whose family members perished, believed that a conviction in this case would not right the wrong. Moussaoui himself expressed a sense of betrayal at his defense team which, he claimed, did not respect or represent his wishes to become a martyr for his cause. He was questioned by authorities before the attacks and of course said nothing. Assuming he knew anything, had he given information he would have betrayed his fellow attackers.

But the patchwork of betrayals didn't end there. One government lawyer was found to have coached prosecution witnesses, thus betraying the rules of U.S. jurisprudence. Much of the public would have felt betrayed if the prosecution's case was found deficient, though, so in a marked departure from accepted procedure that lawyer got away with a reprimand—and the judge, after some anger and an appropriate period of deliberation, allowed the tarnished testimonies to go forward. If Moussaoui were to be executed, the U.S. legal system would have betrayed an innocent man—irrespective of his loudly proclaimed hatred for the United States and its people.

Further, Zacarias Moussaoui was considered by the psychiatrists who examined him to be a paranoid schizophrenic. In court he frequently blurted out his conviction that President Bush would set him free. The U.S. judicial system is supposed to take into account an accused person's mental state; if the person is found guilty, he or she must be remanded to a mental institution rather than prison. But this couldn't be allowed to happen here. Whatever the verdict in this case, some would feel vindicated while others would know that making a man pay with his life for a crime in which he was not involved would be a gross betrayal of justice.

On May 4, 2006, after a week of deliberation, the jurors in the Zacarias Moussaoui case decided his modified guilt. They couldn't prove he'd participated—in fact several of them, as well as many pundits, believed he had little if any involvement—but neither could they absolve him. The Court spared him the death penalty, sending him to prison for life without possibility of parole.

We live in a time in which betrayal—violence in general—is not only twisted by forces of hate, but condoned and even glorified by those same forces. Only the names have been changed, and not to protect the innocent. When invasion and occupation are called liberation and democracy, when taking people's employment is called streamlining the economy, when people are lured to this country to work the jobs we don't want, then hunted and deported when no longer useful, betrayal as we have been taught to identify it is a jigsaw of answerless questions.

In the twenty-first-century United States, public service has almost uniformly become power sold to the highest bidder, a place where the greedy and opportunistic thrive. Betrayal, in its large and small manifestations, has become ordinary currency: the new status quo.

This global geopolitics is refracted as well into a million singular betrayals: children by parents, spouses by one another, anyone by an authority figure he or she trusts. Pharmaceutical companies betray potential customers with misleading advertising and false promises. Politicians betray citizens by using deceptive language to con their constituency and making promises they have no intention of keeping. Banks and brokers use elaborate pyramid schemes to betray their clients. The great betrayals are not possible without the more intimate acts. Everyday person-to-person treachery reflects our "do as I say not as I do" culture.

Betrayal is a map, a sheet of paper upon which many roads may be traced. Some only pay attention to the major highways. Others search out the back roads, the country lanes, and city streets where people live. Complexity is always present, even when not instantly apparent.

Who, we ask, gains from the particular betrayal? Who ends up with the thirty pieces of silver?

CRYSTAL'S GIFT

Imagine walls of massive rock, where two hundred and fifty million years disappear without a trace into something called The Great Unconformity. Think of a river named Colorado, for the deep brown-red of her waters before men built a dam to harness her course. Learn that this section of river now issues from beneath Glen Canyon Dam, keeping a steady forty-eight degrees in contrast with July's hundred-plus-degree heat.

Two hundred and eighty-seven miles of river flow between these canyon walls. Here light moves across shadow, shadow cuts through light. Billions of years of polished black schist are infused with stripes of pink granite, and these glisten richly in the midday sun. Grand Canyon, where the Colorado parts its series of inner gorges, is a geological event that touches the most intimate places of memory.

This is a story about the women who row this river in a world of men. Nine women in particular, who rowed in the summer of 1997, for twenty passengers—also women. I am one of the latter. We have come from different places with varying expectations, some seeking challenge, others quiet retreat. Many of us are long-time friends; others meet for the first time in Flagstaff the night before we put onto the water. We are writers, artists, an anthropologist, a math professor, a filmmaker, a steel worker turned book binder, a special education teacher, nurses, an investment counselor, a builder of houses, massage therapists, a midwife, a muralist and graphics designer. We range in age from our twenties to our sixties.

The boatwomen are our guides. They will reveal the river's mysteries, offering them in manageable pieces, explaining—but never too much or too fast. From their own experience, they will introduce us to the river, and the river to our shy or awestruck tracks.

Our trip leader, Jano, is baptizing her own dory on this trip. In 1997 it is still hard for women to get certified, to accumulate enough trips so they may become licensed to carry passengers. Women row baggage rafts for years before they get to row a boat. Men often show up at one of the companies and are hired on the spot. Once they do obtain their licenses, most boatwomen row rafts; some operate motor rigs. Few row dories, fewer still dories they build themselves.

Jano does just that. She worked on her fifteen-foot rig weekend after weekend, driving in to the company warehouse in Flagstaff from her teaching job on the Navajo reservation. In the construction process, this thirty-one-year-old river guide, writer, and teacher learned to shape and lay the fiberglass decks, mold gunwales of pale ash, attach hardware for the hatch covers, and master the math that brought it all together. In this community dories are traditionally named after places damaged or destroyed by man. Jano's is the Animas, after the Animas River in southern Colorado, now ravaged by industry and development.

At almost fifty, Ote is our oldest woman at the oars. She will be rowing Dark Canyon, in its classic design a sister to Animas. Ote is tall and lithe, sinewy of body, weathered of face. At a critical point along our way, she will give me an image I will not lose: her determination standing and straining as she manages to bring her dory back upriver and in through a fierce eddy line just below the worst of Crystal Rapid.

At mile 98.5, Crystal is the Colorado's most technically difficult rapid—rated a ten plus on the scale of one to ten. A huge hole drops just below its glassy tongue, giant waves crash in every direction, and a treacherous rock garden separates its upper and lower sections. In her capacity as trip leader, Jano decides Crystal is the only one of this river's forty-seven major rapids we passengers will not be permitted to run.

Our guides will take it on in twos, each woman bailing for her sister and then running back along the shore to repeat the process with another boat. We will struggle on foot across the debris field that borders the rapid. The boatwomen tell us there are two eddies, and they will try to make it into the first, thereby avoiding our having to extend an already strenuous hike further down river to the second.

Before attempting this feat, they tie up their boats, climb to a rise of rock and scout what they are about to navigate. One collects dry branches that another tosses into the current, to see which way they go. Then they are ready. Quick hugs and into the boats. We start our trek. One after another, each spot of color approaches the rapid: toylike images far below us in the thunderous river—now visible, now disappearing beneath huge surges of spray. It is all about entering correctly. As if suspended, each dory floats for a moment on the swelling tongue, then plunges into the current.

Only Ote finds herself in position to try for the first eddy. She knows how important it will be for at least one boat to be there to pick up the more physically challenged among us. In her mind failure is not an option. And—every leg and arm muscle taut with the effort—she makes it through. No one else comes close.

But I am going too fast. Ote's accomplishment is still days ahead of us, down river. As we put onto the water at Lee's Ferry, this moment and others of equal drama are yet to come. Now the women finish loading their boats. Elena, who is a public health nurse off-season, will row the Phantom. Mary—graphics designer and artist—laughs as she runs her rough fingers over the cracked gray decks of the Mille Crag Bend.

Although she did not build it, the Mille Crag also belongs to Mary. Its ownership fulfills a long-held dream. No more than a week before our trip the phone call came from Martin Litton, writer, conservationist, founder of Grand Canyon Dories, and grand old man of the Colorado. "You want the Mille Crag?" he asked her, referring to the old Briggs boat stored unused for the past eight years up at his place in Hurricane. "Yes, I do," Mary managed to sputter, caught totally by surprise. On a number of occasions she had asked her friend to sell her this boat. Now: "How much do you want for her?" "What, you rich or something?" The man's gruff laugh accompanied his revelation of the gift.

The Ticaboo is being rowed by Cindell: small, wiry, a high school physical education teacher from Tucson. This is Cindell's first-time rowing passengers the length of the Colorado through Grand Canyon. She has passed up a chance to make a trip with her husband, also a boatman, to participate in this all-female adventure. Our first morning out, one of the other boatwomen suggests a stop at a particular beach. Hanging on the branch of a tree, some two hundred yards from shore, Cindell discovers a ziplock bag containing a lovely turquoise ring: a surprise gift from the man she loves.

Now the women finish packing their boats. Stephanie and Nicole each command a large yellow rubber baggage raft; their helpers are Jenna and Denise. We make our first of many human chains to help load dry bags, sleep kits, and other paraphernalia for sixteen days of life along the river's banks. Everything carried in must come out.

Our life jackets are being fitted now: low and snug. They bear the names of local animals or places. Each of us will remember "Pallid Bat" or "Canyon Wren" or "Nankoweap," so these life-saving devices may remain with us and always fit as they should. After Jano rounds us up for final introductions and a few last-minute safety tips, we group up four to a dory and put into the green water.

The river has been running relatively high at 27,000 cubic feet per second (CFS), issuing from under the dam at a volume and speed that washes some of her rapids out and makes others larger, less predictable. The engineering project was authorized by Congress in 1956 and completed in 1963. Beyond erasing forever magnificent Glen Canyon, it has changed the Colorado from the raging current rowed by Powell in 1869 to the tamer but still unpredictable river it is today.[1]

We are finally on our way. And now the stories begin—about rock strata, sediment, water, and wind: how the Canyon came to be. Stories of the ancient Basketmakers who first inhabited this place, of the Ancestral Puebloans and more recent Hualapai, Havasupai, Hopi, Paiute, and Diné (Navajo). Stories about Powell, Stanton, and others among the early white explorers. The men who first ran this river—in scows, motor craft of various kinds, eventually rafts and dories. And about the very few women linked to Canyon history.

The first were the old-timers' wives and daughters. Although the legends and books do not focus on them, many made enormous sacrifices for the river and shared fully in early explorations. Then came a group of Hollywood models. Requisites were beauty and (just as absurd) an ability to swim; they were hired by the first companies to add glamour to the river's commercialization. Finally, several generations of boatwomen made their way onto the Colorado.

Georgie White was the first, a generation with a single name. For forty years she was the only woman of Grand Canyon river legend, until male resistance began to crumble before female skill—and will. Then came Marilyn, Liz, Suzanne, Connie, and Ellen: the second generation of Colorado River women. Today we are traveling with women of the third generation. They are still pioneers.

"Was that a rapid?" "No, just a riffle." Nervous or relieved laughter can be heard from boat to boat. "How long have you been rowing? Was it hard to break into the man's world of dories?" Our questions come, uncertain at first, the boatwomen's answers also tentative, feeling us out.

Then, as the days unfold, the old stories emerge. There is the geology and the botany of Grand Canyon, how the same huge barrel cactus we saw on yesterday's hike can be seen in a hundred-year-old photograph made on the Stanton Expedition of 1892. There are tales of the Big-horn Sheep, the lizards and snakes and hawks and wrens. Our guides are experienced experts in all these fields.

And there are the human stories: What really happened to the three men on Powell's first expedition who gave up on the endeavor and walked out at what we now call Separation Canyon? Were they murdered by Paiute Indians as the plaque in their honor claims? Did they die of thirst and hunger somewhere along the nonexistent trails? Or were they shot by Mormons who believed them federal agents, a version that has gained credibility with the recent surfacing of a series of old letters?

Then there were Glen and Bessie Hyde, honeymooners who went downriver in a wooden scow in 1928. The few who saw them along the way said the trip was his idea; she was clearly unhappy, being prodded along by her publicity-seeking husband. Why was their boat discovered intact? Why were no bodies ever found?

A boatman on my first river journey, back in 1995, told me that on another trip he and his group were sitting in a circle after dinner one night on one of the Colorado's quiet beaches. He was telling the Bessie and Glen Hyde story. Suddenly a woman in her eighties stood and walked to the center of the circle. "I'm Bessie Hyde," she announced.

The age seemed right, some of the details too. The woman was later questioned by reporters, but proved unwilling to reveal what had happened to Glen or how she had walked out of Grand Canyon. Mute testimony—if true—to what can happen when a man tries to force a woman to do something against her will.

There are plenty of stories about Georgie White, or Georgie

Clark as she was later known. In the mid-1950s she devised a way of linking three big pontoon motor rafts—Georgie's G-rigs, they were called—in order to take large numbers of people downriver at a price they could afford. She was the first woman to run the Colorado commercially, and made the experience accessible to thousands.

But on our trip the stories that most vividly resonate within me are the ones about our own boatwomen, their ordinary and extraordinary lives. These stories are harder to come by; the women tend to talk little about their accomplishments.

Each woman who has wanted to take a dory through Grand Canyon has had to row baggage or cook for these trips an average of six years before being entrusted with a boat and passengers. Ote started rowing in 1976; Elena, Mary, and Jano in the eighties. Cindell has rowed baggage for years; this is her first commercial dory experience.

Can women row dories? In this tradition-bound community the question once challenged women as well as men. For years the answer was not the offhand "of course" it is today. But dory people now agree that women make up in finesse what they may lack in absolute strength. "We learn to read the water really well. Each of us develops a style that works with our body. And then we've had all those years of practice," Mary laughs.

None of the many details of their lives, though, reflects what makes these women seem a breed apart. Rather, it is the solidity of their underlying self-confidence, the sense they embody that if you love something you just naturally go after it. And if you go after it you will do it well. No doubt in these muscular arms as they guide their boats through the water. No ostentation, no bravado or risk for risk's sake.

Now all but one of the baggage rafts have run Crystal. Two dories have sustained severe rock damage and will be mended by their boatwomen when we reach an accessible beach. All that remains is for that last raft to come through. Suddenly there it is. And then those of us watching from the rocky shore look helplessly as it flips like a slip of paper in slow motion, coming down bottom-up upon the waves.

We can see Stephanie's and Nicole's bodies. One woman is clinging to the edge of the raft, the other rushes by some hundred feet in front. They are being carried through the churning rapid at more miles per hour than any of us wants to contemplate. The raft, now a lump of gray instead of its familiar yellow, careens among the rocks.

Ote's dory still bobs alone in the first of Crystal's eddies. We shout down to the boatwomen who have tied theirs up in the second eddy far below: "A flip," we yell, "there's been a flip!" "Shit," I later learn is Jano's first response, "I've got to get those women."

With two passengers sitting in Animas, she wastes no time pulling into the current. She positions herself as the two terrified members of her crew come racing down and, one after the other, pulls them into the dory. Then she manages to grab the overturned raft and bump it to shore.

But this is only the most important part of this rescue. When a dory flips, it is easy to right. Two or three moderately strong women standing on the upturned bottom, arching their backs and pulling on the flip line, can accomplish the task. We have been coached several times in this, given explicit training in how to proceed should our dory succumb to an angry wave.

When a baggage raft goes over, it's a different story. The fully loaded hulk of rubber is heavy and awkward and extremely difficult to return to its upright position. Now the gray mass sits defiant, all our lashed-on gear hidden beneath it in the water. More quickly than any of us could have imagined possible, we have brought the raft alongside a rocky part of the shore. Not really a beach but we had no choice. A few of us stand in the numbing water to keep the wooden boats from crashing against the sharp obstructions or ourselves. Quickly, deftly, the boatwomen rig a series of ropes and pulleys; a rise of jagged rock affords a certain angle of maneuverability.

With more time to struggle with the rigging, twenty-some-odd women would have been enough. But a passing raft trip has stopped to offer assistance. With their power and ours we manage to right the monster. Everything tied on is still there. The bags are wet but none the worse for their long soak, and their contents are safe and mostly dry. Relieved, we make our way a short distance further downriver where we will lunch as the women whose dories have been damaged pull them ashore and plug their holes.

Later that evening I ask Jano, "On a mixed trip what would this day have been like?" "The men would have taken over," she tells me, smiling but with an edge of seriousness in her eyes. "The work would have gotten done of course. But we would have been pushed aside. That's the way it is. When there are men around, the women just don't get a chance to deal with the problems that arise."

But neither is this the end of the incident. Women have our own ways of handling mishap and fear. Jano gathers her crew on a secluded part of the beach, giving the two women who flipped their needed opportunity to debrief, vent, cry, be held. She makes sure they understand it was not their fault. In Grand

Canyon boats flip every day. And Crystal is certainly one of the places where that happens.

A quality these boatwomen share is their deep devotion to passing it on. They love teaching the younger guides, and aspire that each passenger not only experience Grand Canyon to its fullest but come to know her own potential: previously unclaimed strengths, a trust in her body, new powers of observation, the ability to make connections in this harsh desert terrain.

"The one piece of advice I can give you is: go slow." That's Jano in Flagstaff the night before we depart. "Go slow. Look. Listen. Pay attention."

Like precious gifts, these women give us the unequaled beauty of a magical fern-covered slot or the way out of a lifetime of vertigo. They do not offer these experiences lightly but teach us how to acquire them for ourselves. It is not by pushing or extolling that they instruct, but by watching, listening, and being present—always—to offer a hand or point out a foot- or fingerhold.

Gradually we passengers find we need less, appreciate more. Dropping into a slot canyon was a challenge we didn't think we'd meet, but did. Scaling a difficult stretch of rock another. We delight in the little bats that circle above us as we sleep, look closely at the Ringtail Cat tracks appearing at first light around our camp, marvel at the legions of tiny frogs.

The river becomes our companion, friend, source. We drink its filtered water, urinate in its rapidly renovating current, wash clothes in its eddies, cool ourselves or bathe in its shocking temperature, feel its caress against our skin.

In a little more than two weeks, the boatwomen have made it their business to see, really see, each one of us. They have learned our physical and emotional limits and worked to help us stretch — unobtrusively, so that we do not know we are being worked with except perhaps in retrospect.

Before this journey one or another of us might have said we were running the Colorado for the excitement of the rapids or the beauty of the canyon, for the opportunity to spend sixteen days beside walls of rock that are at once ethereal and massive, translucent and imposing, gold orange red and deep violet in moonlight or brilliant sun. We might have explained that we wanted to get away or be in nature or commune with four billion years of life.

What we didn't know was that we would be given the gift of ourselves. This is what these boatwomen offer, each from her unique experience. These women who regularly spend time away from lovers and well-paid work to transport people to the center of the earth — where, if we have looked and listened, we will have found the greatest gift of all: a new belief in our untapped capacity to be and do.

THE PLACE WHERE
COLOR SOUNDS
for Lisa Birman and Max Regan

The line expressing my temperature year to year, place to place, is not accompanied by reassuring beeps on a hospital monitor. It is a lineage. I am my own protagonist and my pulse can be gauged more accurately by its echo against red rock canyon walls than between any doctor's fingers. The line where water and stone meet as the Colorado flows through Grand Canyon. The line, the line. Try to knock it out with a pencil-tip eraser or computer delete button. Try to ignore its music. It always returns. Close your eyes, cover your ears; I'm still coming through loud and clear.

Color brings it all together, gives it name. The first time I discovered that color is more than color to me, that hearing a particular sound or seeing words, letters, or numbers in differing hues is a peculiarity I share with others, was several years back in a dentist's waiting room. I was thumbing through *Smithsonian* magazine and came upon an article on synesthesia. Random House defines the condition (talent?) as "a sensation produced in one modality when a stimulus is applied to another, as when the hearing of a certain sound induces the visualization of a certain color."

I know it is more complex than that. Synesthesia can best be understood as adventure, exploration, the mind's refusal to compartmentalize, a piercing of membranes between the senses. A constant linkage. The art and science of making connections. Magic. Some people with synesthesia smell music, others see sound. For some, touch and taste are involved. A person generally experiences insistent crossover, one sense morphing into another. Like the cross-dresser or, more profoundly, the woman or man wrongly assigned at birth, who must seek a return to core identity because anything less is death. It's that important, that necessary to survival.

For me it is about color. I hear a sound, word, letter, and that signifier is accompanied or represented by a particular tint, even a very precise hue. My own name, Margaret, and so also the letter *M*, are a full rich red. Never tilting toward pink or orange but red as red should be. I have sometimes likened it to dark chocolate as opposed to its pastier milk variety. Hovering just beneath the surface. Velvet-skinned yet determined.

The way this particular red fits the letter *M*, though, is not characteristic of the way in which color stands in for words in my experience. Perhaps it is different because it belongs to me: moving from center out. The question of hue is also where ease of explanation breaks down, because although some sounds always evoke the same color, others do not.

On a cloudy day, in a room that is too hot, inching along a mountain trail that clings precipitously to the side of a cliff, or in a different time zone, a sound or word may assume a slightly different shade or another color entirely. Is it Fahrenheit or Centigrade, pound or kilo, mile or kilometer? The differences are important, and this may confuse the casual observer, sometimes even leading him to doubt my claim. Why isn't water always silvery violet? Are you sure you're not making this up?

There is also the matter of opaqueness versus translucence. And this latter may or may not denote transparency. What we hide from others or ourselves. What we want the world to know.

You say a lover once accused you of being "geographically unstable." Where is the elegance of a physical or mathematical equation on the map of nature's pulsing heart? Everywhere, I tell you, everywhere.

Come on now: think shape-shifter. Think draining color from a map's face. We are taught Mercatur from elementary school on up. Back when I was a professor I would bring a Peters Projection to the first meeting of each new class. Mapa Mundi in another dimension, ready to astonish and reveal. On the Peters the larger land masses are correctly immense, the smaller dutifully minute, distancing us from that Eurocentric world vision in which the "civilized" countries of the North are erroneously outsized in relation to those of the more "primitive" South. At first the students floundered. Some laughed. Then they got it. He who conquers wields an insidious pen.

Color accompanies men and women into battle, picks them up from defeat, warns them that victory may not always translate as winning. Leonel Rugama was a young poet and revolutionary in the Nicaragua of the 1960s. He joined the Sandinistas to fight against Somoza's half-century dictatorship; and died alone, before his twenty-first birthday, in a house surrounded by dozens or maybe hundreds of soldiers. Rugama once said most Nicaraguans were so poor, so lacking in hope that they dreamed in black and white. "When our country is free," he is reported to have predicted, "everyone will dream in color."

What color is patriotism? Hope? Fear? Emptiness? Risk? Courage? Compassion?

Don't tell me white.

Time is also part of the equation. Time zones do battle with the body's senses. In ancient times, when most people lived all their years within relatively small areas, they weren't faced with the uprooting and repositioning that extreme mobility demands of our internal clocks today. The child at Machu Picchu, Kiet Seel, or Rapa Nui knew she lived at the center of the world. She could lift her hands in any direction and feel the sun or rain. Even the aging immigrant in his New York City ghetto, circa late 1800s, had no need to stray from his three- or four-block neighborhood, his language, his comfort zone. Hands made for work moved the dominoes across a wooden tabletop. Other hands washed, just kept on washing.

I am not talking about migration here, which offers a different palette. Once it was brown: early peoples streaming north to south and east to west in search of a place to settle. Their animals came with them, providing company and food. They traveled to find better land, conditions, life. Today's migrations wear the colorlessness of pain, forced by violence and hunger, war and fictitious division, and stumble on by the millions into the charcoal gray of approaching night.

Between individuals time can turn life on its head. I once saw an art object composed of two identical wall clocks hung side by side exactly seven feet above the floor. They were severe in their plain round faces, black rims, and stark black numbers. A red second hand ponderously circled each. The clocks hung on a museum wall, one just touching the other, forming a perfect figure eight. Only their ticking differed. Although both kept time in determined forward motion, one's rhythm was slightly slower than the other's. Relentless and bereft, for the clocks represented the artist's tribute to his lover who was dying of AIDS. One day the slower clock would stop. The artist knew it, and his viewers felt it in every one of their body's senses.[1]

Each time a great silver bird carries me across longitudinal lines, I must carefully reposition each cog in the wheel that allows me to see, walk, run. Run, Jane, run; but never too far from home. Sometimes our ability to cross time zones like the wind tricks our senses and wreaks havoc with the arithmetic of our minds. When I flew from Albuquerque to Rapa Nui, that tiny island in the south-central Pacific, I did so via Tahiti. Four hours lost going west, then gained once more after reaching the apex of that day's triangle and heading back east. Finally, it was the same time in Hanga Roa as it was in Albuquerque, latitudes surprising the best-laid plans of Melatonin and spirit. As I gazed in early morning light at those giant stone statues, their patient backs to the sea, knowing the sun was simultaneously rising at home built a bridge I cross again and again.

The tree of our living has many and varied branches, some vulnerable and easily snapped, others stout: dug in for the long haul. Some stretch skyward, others bow to earth or even bury themselves for a timeless night of regeneration where branch morphs to root, and direction is far more difficult to discern. Color codes these twists and turns. So does sound.

Sound as language: a particular configuration of inflection, intonation, meaning. Position of tongue against teeth, lips pursing and parting, that mysterious cave where slides and clicks can sometimes be heard, lungs holding and releasing breath. I was born into English, a raucous New York English my mother thought uncouth. The first time I ever heard that word — uncouth — was in connection with my less than genteel pronunciation, an accent she deemed lower-class and fought against for years. I held on for dear life.

It would be decades before I understood the self-hate implicit in her plea. She had suffered from anti-Semitism as a child and thought shunning her own Jewishness could protect her children. In my generational failure to see her in her time and place, I wanted her to have known she had other choices. To her ear, my accent gave us away. As a child my rejection of the lie was instinctive. I didn't know why I nurtured that way of speaking she hated so much, only that it was an important piece of my identity, something I would not let go of. Lonely shame pulled my mother down. A community of courage supported my option to stand.

I was born into English, then as a young woman leapt a broad canyon into Spanish. In Spain, Mexico, Cuba, and Nicaragua I embraced that other sound — with its relevant range of color — and for a while it became my home. As I had cried out in English while giving birth to my son, I cried out in Spanish when my three daughters were born. And I acquired political consciousness in that language as well, such that even today a discussion about class or profit motive spills from me most easily in Vallejo's sweet southern vowels. Marxism in Spanish, we liked to say.

Back on my childhood landscape, in the light of this New Mexican desert or in the canyons that call my name, a deeper awareness was born. I dance along the lines of race and gender, climb out onto the branches of cultural difference, explore the busy intersections of memory lost and gained, and revel in love in accents bequeathed me by Williams, Rich, and Harjo.[2] The colors are right where they've always been. My fingers know their hues.

Almost a quarter century ago, when Barbara and I fell in love, our differing use of language threatened the incipient bond. She had been taught to think long before uttering a word that might come back to taunt or scar, or bring on an instant beating. Torture—there is no other word for what she survived—drew her face down, pressed her lips together, shattered her heart. I spoke and then reflected or not on what I'd said. Anything could be explained, reiterated, retrieved, changed. Process was everything. Eventually trust's colors flooded our need and saved us from ourselves. Now Barbara's shattered heart is almost whole, a rich cream.

Today I ask myself what phases of the moon color and time move through, not in a single life but in a lineage of lives: generations where the very old, women of childbearing age, men who father those children, and the youngest who come rocketing into the world, ricocheting through the birth canal to receive what we have prepared for them. I am thinking of the Palestinian people, pushed from their land more than half a century ago, cherishing keys to houses they can no longer inhabit, struggling, always struggling, to reclaim origin and place.

Or the successive generations of Tibetans who, just as long ago, began losing their culture, language, and identity: "more precious than their lives," in the words of the Dalai Lama.[3] In Tibet, Chinese officials boast about a "great wall of stability." Israel's wall, crisscrossing occupied Palestine, shreds people's lives every day. Right here in my own U.S. American Southwest, the wall attempting to keep southern migrants from penetrating this territory we have stolen from them uses hunger and thirst as well as the weaponry of war to abort time, wipe color from the human map.

The word *wall* is a dark purple. The word *bridge* is sometimes yellow, sometimes blue-green.

Surely color, multiplied by hundreds of thousands, possesses a different depth and intensity than color reflected in the pupil of a single eye. Surely time stretches and compresses about shoulders, against temples and breasts, in a different rhythm for multitudes than for the individual.

Color and time threaten the earth itself in ways we see clearly today. We ourselves change the palette, rewind the clock. Will we come together, turn the walls to bridges before it's too late?

My Losses

Eight months short of my seventieth birthday I wake up one morning, the word *loss* assaulting my sleep-shuttered lids. The letters are impressive eighteen-point Bodoni Bold.[1] Sleep-crumblies, luscious as scabs but easier to flick away, are no obstacle to those letters; they keep coming in a rhythm that quickens my pulse. I close, then reopen, my eyes.

Still coming.

All day I imagine a neat accounting: my list of losses. I'll make such a list, I tell myself, just as soon as I put in some writing time, finish my morning stint on the treadmill, take a shower, run to the bank and post office, grab a few things at the market, cook. After lunch. After all the day's tasks are checked off. After, always after. Until the Bodoni Bold fills my vision completely.

The nudging has become a thunderous pulse, impossible to ignore.

Time to make that list.

Only after allowing myself to contemplate immediate loss—no more darkroom, for example, where I never failed to experience exhilaration as I coaxed clean whites and true blacks up through the developer—do I remember my definitive losses: the people I loved, those who accompanied moments or years of my journey, those whose lives intersected at length or briefly with my own.

Sam Jacobs, my first husband. Sad young rich boy, hiding childhood hurt and baffled ego behind blustering outbursts of self-righteous impulse. Talented, outrageous. Our painful union ended never too soon. Many years past our marriage, after I'd finished reading poems to a Santa Barbara audience of several hundred, I noticed a lone woman still seated in the empty auditorium. Once everyone else had left, she rose and introduced herself: "I'm Sam Jacob's widow," she said. "He spoke about you often." I knew Sam had died young, but not how. His widow explained it had been a heart attack in his early forties. She told me they had two daughters and theirs was a happy union. "He'd grown up by the time we met. He always felt badly about his time with you."

If I weren't making this compilation of loss, there would be little or no place for Sam in my memory. For a few brief years the center of my life, now he is almost irrelevant. A shifting of emphasis that still astonishes.

Jason Harvey comes into focus now. A lover during my New York years, mid to late 1950s, and one of the few in whom tenderness and respect were always present. Jason designed lamps. I thought of him as a creator of light. He and I were together, briefly, during my pregnancy with Gregory. My son's middle name does him honor. Thirty years later a letter from Jason's son tells of his father's death. "He talked about you," he wrote. "He would have wanted you to know."

Giving birth to my son defines those New York years. During our five days in Manhattan General's grim forty-bed maternity ward—filled with other women like myself: poor, uncounted, dependent upon public health facilities—Ammon Hennacy came to visit, bearing a single perfect peach. Ammon was a Catholic Worker, tall and thin with thick white hair, unique among protestors at more than a few political demonstrations. Decades later I learned of his death in Salt Lake City, where he'd gone to found a Catholic Worker House. Ammon was my introduction to politics not just articulated but lived.

I associate other losses with those New York years. Al Held, a fine painter with whom I had a short and mostly unrequited romance. News of his death among the *New York Times* obituaries one morning produced a shiver of pain. Seymour Krim, who used to say that if both of us remained single we should think about marrying and caring for one another in old age. Lifetimes later Seymour chose death when the terminal illness he suffered became too much of an impediment to living. Those who knew him better than I said the note he left was matter-of-fact.

My son's father, the poet Joel Oppenheimer, is also gone: dead of cancer in 1988.

Joel's death produced a poem I continue to read to audiences now and then:

We are poets who walked briefly
in each other's lives,
grow old in New Hampshire, New Mexico,
our children and their children
testing the words we leave behind.

Always in present tense. When it was his time to go, Joel's wife called me in New Mexico and I called Gregory in Paris. Our son was able to speak to his biological father by phone, say good-bye.

Elaine de Kooning died in 1989, victim of a lifetime of smoking laced with bravado. In Elaine the world lost a great painter and I a lifelong mentor and friend, a woman to whom I owe much of what I am. Brilliance, courage, abandon, and risk are the words that come most quickly to mind. Femme fatal drawn in the powerful lines of abstract expressionism. Her warm and stalwart sister, Marjorie, didn't outlive her long enough to finish editing those mystery journals so many still want to read.

Dear friends from my years in Mexico, Laurette Séjourné and Arnaldo Orfila, both departed in the 1990s. He first, she some years later. He was more than one hundred. She tried leaving earlier but family and friends kept stifling her decision, denying her the dignity of that single moment she might finally have controlled completely.

In the early 1960s, shortly after Gregory and I arrived in Mexico, Laurette started taking us to her dig at Teotihuacán: Palace of the Butterflies. Arnaldo later became my first editor at Siglo XXI, the publishing house he founded with the support of Mexico's artists and intellectuals after the government ousted him from El Fondo de Cultura Económica. In the early '60s, in the opinion of Mexico's government, El Fondo's publication of C. Wright Mills's *Listen, Yankee!* and *The Children of Sánchez* by Oscar Lewis put a reading public too intimately in touch with U.S. designs on Latin America and Mexico's own reality of poverty.

Delicate Clara—what was her last name? Oh yes, Hernández. I remember her as a slight wisp of a woman. She died in

1969. Cause of death: an auto accident provoked by her hotshot boyfriend driving his Alfa Romeo one hundred twenty miles an hour over Cuba's broken highways. For a week the hospital kept us guessing; we wanted to hope she would survive. Then fantasy went up in flames and I sat with other friends at the funeral home, a long sad night. Clara's mother grieved back and forth, back and forth, in one of those high-backed rockers that populate Cuban wakes. She never stopped tapping her foot against the marble floor.

Roque Dalton was wrenched from us in 1975. The news came, unreal at first, via Mexico from the jungles of El Salvador. We all knew our friend had returned to his country to fight. What none of us could have imagined was that a jealous faction in his own organization would torture and murder him as well as another, younger, combatant. This wouldn't be the last betrayal among revolutionary cadre in El Salvador; in time it would show itself to be a terrible flaw, a blight on the popular movement. Years later one of Roque's sons interviewed the man who tortured his father to death: a courageous document exuding dignity. Today the murderer lives in Mexico. He says he is sorry for his youthful excess.

Heroine of the Cuban revolution, my friend Haydée Santamaría took her own life in 1980. News of her death came close to midnight. We walked to the funeral home, just blocks from our seaside apartment, to find it already crowded with people wanting to pay their respects. Standing room only. Someone asked if I would take a turn in the changing honor guard. As I stood by her side for those few moments of surreal communion, I glanced down at Haydée's reconstructed face, expressionless; at the delicate hands arranged across her breast. People whispered betrayal in love, but surely that alone could not have explained her final decision: a bullet in the mouth while her children played downstairs. Later, in the early morning hours, Roque's son Jorge fell into my arms. We held one another in silence.

Because of her suicide Haydée's body was laid out at the funeral home rather than in Revolution Square where the country's heroes were given their official farewells. The Communist Party, like the Catholic Church, doesn't look favorably on suicide—the first believing its members' lives belong to the Party while the second say theirs owe allegiance to God. But on that sad Havana night a people's loud indignation forced a change of venue; Haydée was suddenly moved, claiming her rightful place in earth reserved for heroes and martyrs. This similarity in dogma between Communism and Catholicism would revisit me later around another pair of losses.

El Salvador's incestuous treachery continued with the murder of Comandante Ana María, second-in-command of her country's revolutionary army. One night, at her rear-guard hideaway in Managua, someone stabbed her sleeping body more than eighty times. When Caetano Carpio, her only superior in the struggle, arrived to pronounce the funeral eulogy, details of the crime began to unravel. He was arrested and put in prison, where he ended his own life a few days later. Although I didn't know Ana María personally, her murder haunted me for years. I still sometimes wake from dreams of her ravaged body.

A disagreement about that murder was the last conversation I would have with my friend Rini Templeton, the profoundly generous woman and great people's artist who died not much past her fiftieth birthday and alone in a rooftop maid's room in Mexico City: I accepted the Sandinista version of events, she believed Carpio innocent, a victim of struggles she said I didn't understand.

Rini's body wasn't found for more than a week. Drink and exhaustion probably contributed to her death; there was no evidence of violence. Her clean energetic drawings, reflecting almost every struggle of those years, still show up on flyers and banners, book covers and cards. Today I wear a turquoise bracelet she gave me almost half a century ago.

Emma was her real name, but Ana Herrera was the one with which she signed her uniquely intelligent commentaries in the newspapers and magazines we read back then. Ana was the first of the Latin American journalists in the circles I knew—even the first of the women journalists—to inject a measure of feminist sensibility when addressing the issues that concerned us. She had moved on to Allende's Chile by the time she, her husband, and infant daughter were riding in a Volkswagen Beetle hit by another car. She threw her body around her child: a mother's protective instinct. Her husband lived; so did their baby. Ana breathed and ate and made unintelligible sounds for a few more years, dead in all but the coroner's report. When a few years later I needed a pseudonym for some articles I was writing, I took "Ana" in tribute to her.

Carlos María Guttiérez's prison poems touched me deeply. His was the last manuscript of more than one hundred and twenty I read for Cuba's Casa de las Américas poetry contest in the summer of 1970. Another of the five judges and I immediately knew this had to be the winning book. Our strategy for getting the other three on board was urgent and to no small degree devious. Later Carlos María and I became friends. I translated his *Prison Diary* into English. Many years later he succumbed to the residual damage from the torture he'd suffered while writing those poems.

Teddi Borrego died from leukemia and, years later, our friend

Susan Geiger also lost her battle to the disease. They both fought valiantly. Sometimes I try to imagine how complicated fighting valiantly has to be, how it must require the effort of a lifetime to stay alive until embracing death becomes the wiser comfort. Acknowledgment of the turning point. I think about how the yearnings of loved ones often get in the way of the dying process, how important it is that we allow those we care about to make their exit gracefully, even as a part of us goes with them.

Tede Matthews was my first close friend—though hardly the last—to die from AIDS, the pandemic that has marked our generation. Months before Tede's death I saw him at a reading in San Francisco. Before I could stop myself I exclaimed on how thin he looked. He prolonged our hug as he told me why. Several AIDS victims I've known have chosen to end their suffering rather than allow it to destroy them piece by piece. Others, with a privileged access to new drug cocktails, have beaten the odds for survival. For many, these cocktails brought another kind of death: when the preparation for dying suddenly turned a corner and the stricken and their loved ones had to contemplate life once more.[2] Some burdened with the disease walk bravely through the flames of shame and speak or write about their experience. A multicolor quilt, now too vast to be unfolded in any public place, testifies to the richness of hundreds of thousands of lives.

Nancy Macdonald, my old friend and the woman for whom I worked in the 1950s at New York City's Spanish Refugee Aid, died without my being aware of her passing. I never got to say good-bye. Perhaps this was because we grew apart when I embraced the Cuban revolution. Nancy, out of her horror at Stalin's crimes, became a determined anti-communist. She believed I had gone over to the dark side.

Nguyen Phuc, or Fernando as we called him in Cuba, was in some ways a similar loss. I also heard of his death too long after the fact. We were close throughout the years I taught him English in Cuba, remained close I know. But his Vietnamese Communist Party forbid contact with foreigners, and after he returned to Hanoi I never heard from him again. I'm still not sure why, but coming to know that a close friend has been gone for months or years without personally being aware of the moment of death produces a certain rawness stumbling forward.

I had followed my friend Joan Kelly's struggle with cancer and took solace in her husband's letter telling me her condition had taken a turn for the better. So I was stunned a few weeks later when another friend came up to me at a 1982 gathering in Mexico City and spoke of Joan's recent death. The news struck with shattering force. An even greater shock engulfed me when, waiting for a flight at Miami's airport, I opened the *New York Times* and saw among the obituaries a large photograph of my friend Helen Rodríguez. I remember emitting a small cry, almost dry of breath. Helen's brilliance seemed equaled by her radiant health; I hadn't known she was ill.

Saralee James. I think of her every time I look at her amazing photograph of the Eskimo woman and three children riding an all-terrain vehicle in the windswept cold of the high central Arctic. Like so much of her work, it's a tiny print that wields a huge impact. Saralee was a dear friend and fine photographer whose life ended in an automobile accident. She taught me a lot, including a reverence for the safety and well-being of the nonhuman species. Saralee's brother Arnold Belkin was also a friend: a Mexican painter, dead of cancer in midlife as well. For those who do not live beyond their fifties or sixties, of course, midlife is end time.

Enriqueta Goodson, Julie Nichamin, Ramoncito Feliciano: all died from that horror that slowly eats the mind, burdening with years of deterioration the person unfortunate enough to have the disease. Queta's Alzheimer's came at the end of a full life but didn't want to let her go. Ramon's was early-onset, turning a vibrant political activist to a body gradually disappearing into the recesses of a New Orleans nursing home. I remember Ramoncito, wiry and alert, from 1978 when he did security during a talk of mine in Boston. Raving members of the terrorist group Alpha 66 attacked anyone who spoke publicly and favorably about the Cuban revolution.

Julie's illness, also early-onset, was unique. The brilliant political activist became a walking phantom, eventually taken in by Cuban generosity and dying in one of the island's many sanctuaries for people with problems like hers. Unique because, as I later learned, she inherited the curse from her grandfather, the man whose surname became synonymous with the disease.

My father left us in 1994. He too suffered from Alzheimer's, but his was a more rapid decline than most and almost gentle in its evolution. I think of his passing as a soft rain. What wasn't gentle was Mother's inability or unwillingness to care for him during his last months and weeks. Dad was alone, abandoned by the woman he adored, seemingly only semiconscious of what was happening. My brother, Barbara, and I brought him to Mother's apartment to die. She moved out. The fine cellist Joanna de Keyser, my brother's first wife and long close to Dad, came to play him a couple of short pieces. He left this world a few days later. I often remember one of our last cogent conversations, in which I said "I love you" and he responded "Ditto." I still miss him with an intensity that causes me to tremble.

Mother died twelve years later. One Sunday she attended a

concert with my brother. He said she seemed to enjoy herself. On Monday, when I made my daily telephone call, I could hear the cough. Are you all right? I asked. She admitted to coughing up blood, but when I wondered out loud if we should call her doctor, amended the admission: "Did I really say that? No, no, that was weeks ago." By Tuesday medical attention couldn't be avoided. She was admitted to the hospital with congestive heart failure, a bad case of pneumonia, and—as it later turned out—a blood infection.

Mother understood she was dying and made the decision to have only palliative care. She didn't want to suffer, she said, and wanted us with her: easy enough requests. For two days she received an unbroken string of visits from friends, telephone calls from grandchildren and great-grandchildren. As she had done for my father, Joanna also played the cello for her. On Thursday Mother asked me to remind her of all those who had called or been to visit, and showed sincere appreciation of each person's good-bye. "No more, though," she said, "it's enough." By Friday she was sleeping most of the time and she died that afternoon—accompanied by my brother John, Joanna, Barbara, and me. We all talked to her—some with words we had been unable to bring forth before. Barbara played her Indian flutes. In the week before her death, our mother had finally taken back her life.

Awkwardly, I am the family matriarch now.

My dear old friend Jack Levine died during one of many revisions of this narrative. He had been battling cancer for years, left a grieving wife and two beautiful young daughters. Jack propelled his life in a dogged reversal of the conventional journey. A fine political lawyer, he gave up litigation because it demanded qualities of macho aggressiveness he didn't like in himself. He became a beautiful photographer, made films, wrote. Every minute of his long dying was a praise song to living.

Michael Maggio, an immigration lawyer and friend, also left during a rewrite of this piece. February 10, 2008, following a ten-month battle with cancer. Brilliant at what he did and committed to justice as few I've known, he took on the tough cases: the Central American mother who wanted to reunite her family, the tortured who wanted extradition for his torturer, the Cuban child held by raucous relatives in Miami. After 9/11 Michael represented dozens of Middle Eastern men and women who sought entrance to the United States. He also cooked up a mean Italian pasta, brought people together, was generous with his expertise and a constant presence for those who needed it. He represented me when the U.S. government threatened deportation because of opinions expressed in some of my books. Were it not for him, I might be somewhere else today.

Otto-René Castillo, Javier Heraud, Leonel Rugama, Rodolfo Walsh, Paco Urondo, Carlos Fonseca, José Benito Escobar, and so many others: all ambushed or gunned down or burned alive by an enemy that still punishes tenderness with an overkill of cruelty.

Walter and Lillian Lowenfels, Meridel LeSueur, George Wald, Mario Benedetti, Don Petersen, Audre Lorde, Bella Abzug, Lucy Ann Warner, Milton Resnick, Gloria Anzaldúa, June Jordan, Robert Creeley, Fred Pfeil. Artists, political activists, friends. Losses that dance about me as I write, press in then retreat, calling my name.

And the disappeared—those dead whose deaths bear the marks of a particularly Latin American, particularly twentieth-century, horror, conceived and executed to punish not only the victims but also their families, communities, and nations. Thirty thousand in a single country. Five in a single family. These are losses that turn the living mad, robbed as they are of the relative closure even a broken body brings. I mourn Rodolfo in this way, and Roque—even when eventually we were able to piece together details of the latter's murder.

Some nights I sink into restless sleep mourning the thousands, the tens perhaps hundreds of thousands of disappeared. Not having known them each in life doesn't diminish the magnitude of their loss. Like the victims of the Nazi Holocaust, the Armenian genocide, the Vietnamese whose names are not on the Wall. Like the thousands of Palestinians murdered by Israelis and hundreds of Israelis murdered by Palestinians. The more than one hundred thousand dead to date in the travesty the United States still perpetrates across Iraq. The three thousand dead on September 11, 2001. Or the thousands of young U.S. soldiers still being sacrificed in George W. Bush's "preemptive" wars.

Loss even punctuates the death of the heavy blond woman whose name I cannot retrieve, blown apart mid-1980s by a bomb meant for others at a jungle press conference in Costa Rica. We'd met in Nicaragua a year or two earlier. I'd found someone to care for her young son so she could work, exchanged a bit of unremembered conversation. For a while the blond woman would come to me in the night, but only when, waking from sleep, I would have gone to the kitchen for a snack. She would sit on the edge of the counter, her pudgy legs dangling, and warn me about getting too fat to run.

There are losses that are not literal deaths, such as the awkward but often no less painful turning away of a beloved friend. For reasons unspoken she erases you from her life. You ask what has happened and are met with continued silence. You may even beg. And there is only that dual punishment, hanging heavy as rain-filled clouds, of the rejection itself and the refusal to tell you why. I suffer several such losses. They are with me almost every day.

And what of those I have forgotten, names and faces lost forever in my disintegrating memory? Like the man in Elie Wiesel's *Night*, who told his fellow concentration camp inmates that he couldn't go on, and asked only that they recite Kaddish for him—and Wiesel's confession that they, in their own misery, forgot—I may be forgetting people who meant a great deal to me when they lived.

Every one of them a world, these men and women—the remembered and unremembered. Death being the ultimate divider, they won't return. Some fell in the struggle for justice, until that struggle itself died—or, battered to its minimal expression, seems as good as dead. As painful a loss as any and harder to talk about.

Harder to talk about because for my generation the loss of a socialist alternative wasn't merely a political loss. The year 1989 marked more than the beginning of the end of socialism in our world: societies committed to equality and justice, and achieving both to varying degrees. It didn't only mean an end to oppositional balance, the beginning of criminal hegemony.

The loss of revolutionary struggle signaled a multilayered defeat, a complex global turning away from values of justice and fairness and hope. Those of us involved in that struggle no longer had a purpose larger than ourselves. We lost our compass, our north star, our point of daily reference. We were forced to look at who we are as individuals, our intimate needs and desires. And we weren't prepared for what we saw.

It was a major identity shift. We lost the idea that health, literacy, and work are rights deserved by every human being. We lost the notion of an internationalism that sends teachers and doctors and technicians of every sort to countries that need their service; with no reward but the satisfaction of a job selflessly done. We lost the confidence that comes with believing we can change the world. We lost a generous cross-border culture.

We lost the Cuban ration book that tested our ingenuity and bored us with monotonous menus but assured every child, adult, and old person enough to eat. Those little mounds of rice on the plate, equal before each waiting fork. People's justice, meted out by neighbors: personal and real. Little Ximena's rebuilt ear. My own kidney. Robert's knee. All health services that were readily available and free, many of them life-saving.

Beside these losses, the end of my career as a black-and-white photographer seems insignificant at best, almost sordid in its irrelevance. Yet this is not a contest. My list has no order of importance, no columns where losses are entered by category, rated most or least meaningful.

"On a scale of zero to ten, with ten being the most painful, how much would you say it hurts?" "Well," I say, "I have a pretty high tolerance for pain. What requires heavy-duty painkillers for many doesn't get an aspirin from me. So if I say three or four or seven, how can you know what that means?" The nurse looks at me, annoyed. "I'm not asking you to compare your pain with others,'" she says, "but rate it according to your own experience." "I do not understand the question's usefulness," I begin to protest again, then stop. "Maybe an eight," I say.

Even before we decide to leave the house in the foothills, we turn my darkroom into a guest bedroom. By then I hadn't worked in it for more than a year. The decision seems easy enough; as is my custom, I don't look back. Digital photography has won me over and I am busy teaching myself PhotoShop. It feels good to be rid of those noxious chemicals, so hard on my poor emphysema-wracked lungs. But, oh that image rising in the tray! Oh the nuanced expression on a face half in shadow but detailed enough to hold the viewer's eye! Those absolute blacks and gleaming whites: beautiful challenge of the perfect print. And my own way of keeping the departed close.

At least today, then, number one on my loss list would be working in the darkroom. Long hours, no music or anything else intruding upon my concentration. How many times did you ask me if I wouldn't like a little radio or CD player for that small dark space? How many times did I say thank you but no? Silence and darkness around me, holding me fast. Alone with my negatives, chemicals, and the memory of that particular depression of the shutter. What I saw, felt, understood. A gesture stopped in time.

And then, in the darkroom, just enough and not a fraction of a second more exposure to light. Light's intensity: measured in the precision of an old Leitz enlarger. My hand moving between light and paper, fingers fluttering. Laws of science and creative risk.

The nightmare began ten or twelve years back, repeated variations on a singular fear. I am somewhere, anywhere, camera raised to eye level, mind adjusting for meaning, right hand preparing for action. Not a second too soon. No waiting either.

But when the pad of my right forefinger presses down on the shutter button, I do not hear the familiar click. I keep pressing harder, insistent, desperate. Nothing happens. Frustration encourages force. I grind my finger into the button. The moment is gone. The camera itself begins to disintegrate in my hand. Pieces slough off in every direction. Still I try to rescue the film, now unfurled from a broken machine, spooled beneath me, emptied of image. No use. Slowly, slowly and with palpable horror, I return to wakeful consciousness.

It is not this shot I have lost, but the photographer's skill itself. My craft, its practiced rightness. The dream represents a loss only beginning to unfold. I cannot yet see around its edges, am afraid to guess its dimension.

Number two on my list might be the tons—yes, literally thousands of pounds—of books and papers I wave away with a flick of my hand as we prepare to move from a large house to one much smaller. Rooms lined with books. One long hall, its length of floor- to-ceiling shelves: all full. Books arranged in careful order, according to subject matter, or alphabetically by author's name. Books to which I go in luxurious anticipation when I need a name, date, place, piece of information, or simply a wonderful read.

My beloved brother, who deals in old and rare books, spends every day of one whole week going through each volume page by page, removing the occasional pressed flower, startled book-mark, snapshot, or long-forgotten note, separating those books to be donated to libraries from those to be sold or given away. Since that divestment I occasionally seek a particular title, want to bury myself in its pages, extract a misplaced clue, reread a dedication—Roque's red scrawl, for example, on the title page of *Miguel Marmol*, his acknowledgment of my help in typing the manuscript for that first edition.

Nothing like real longing, though. Nothing like grief.

Number three on my loss list—again, please don't look for meaning in this order—would be memory. Memory for the necessary word, end of sentence, a person's name, that important call I needed to make. Remembering the final exchange around a particular issue, not just the next to last.

Small things.

Still confident in my larger memory, I never worry about remembering that I love you. My children's open mouths and eyes, the feel of each curling against my body, will always accompany me. My belief system remains rock solid. It's the details I've lost, the pieces and their connective tissue.

Time. Fear of taking too much or not enough. Soft echoes of my mother or first-grade teacher scolding, "Hurry up, we'll be late." Or "You're wasting time." My insistence with my own children: "It's worth that extra couple of hours to get it right." Whatever it may have been.

With more years lived than remaining, time moves palpably faster. By late afternoon I wonder where the day went, what I have to show for having taken it on. Seasons succeed one another before I have fully engaged the one just passed.

Right now each day of the week collapses into the next as if from a very high precipice. Wind howls about my face, eyes water, mouth feels parched: desert-dry. My body descends with the wind, spinning faster in its downward thrust. I glimpse the canyon floor below, but it doesn't get any closer.

Of course I know that time's apparent speed-up is an illusion. But why does it quicken my breath, fill my eyes with such an array of images? Is it because the blood runs more slowly and so much more of what I make and do is recognizable in its repetition? Or is it because as I age I am less likely to be caught off guard, startled out of my routine?

Chaos is precious, unpredictability a flower to be nurtured.

Hiking. I have lost this too, as daily practice and joy. I started late, which may be one of the reasons I loved it so intensely. Some of my greatest discoveries have come at the end of a difficult hike. After encouraging me, my love, in appreciation of the natural world, the desert—my first landscape—and its inhabitants, your own feet fail, or more accurately your knees. You no longer hike and I have been lazy about looking for another to share my explorations of canyon and river bed, mountain trail and journey to ancient community.

Your favorite sport these days is biking. I haven't yet sold my bike and it sometimes taunts me from its hook on the shed's back wall. But when I think of riding, my right ankle explodes out of the toe clip once more. Again it is that bright day in the fall of 1992 on a sunflower-lined country road. A fear of lost balance invades my body. And this is yet another loss: the easy balance of youth.

My body's physical losses can be tabulated, easily checked off in time and place. All those pounds I gained as I aged, and those I lost, finally, when health knocked gluttony down a peg—the latter unfortunately fewer than the former. I lost my left kidney in 1969. Lost the soft lining of my lungs to fifteen years of smoking and more than that of other people's smoke. After the biking accident, I lost the bones in my right ankle, replaced now with metal plates and screws.

Perfect vision, perfect teeth and gums, inviolability of place: all these left during the years of my immigration case, 1985 to 1989. More dramatically I lost my trademark head of wild gray hair, waking one morning to find it limp and thin, swatches of scalp clearly visible. I quickly traded it, then, for the shortest of cuts. Even height has been lost, imperceptibly, so that when my proud five feet five- and-a-half inches reduced to five feet three, I grieved.

Who knows where it will end. I think of my father's eyes, weeks before his death, sunken and tiny, disappearing behind tired folds of paper-thin skin.

And oh, how I mourn the loss of my children. They are still my children, of course—even in their forties and beyond—but I have lost their closeness, need, day-to-day conversation. The changing expressions on a face, relaxed interaction rather than expectation of imposition, times together not classified as visits. Visits: too often those largely fictitious times framed by beginnings and ends and unfamiliarity and tension. One cannot lose one's children. Not really. But living in different time zones makes for staccato communication.

Perhaps what I have lost is the memory of my young children as I have gained their adult selves. Certainly I have gained the grandchildren who populate my intimate horizon. Still, I grieve the loss of that closeness, generation to generation, as the human beings to whom I gave birth bring their own progeny along.

Vast geographies draw a curtain on vulnerability and questions. The girl child—young woman now—whose face, especially her eyes, evokes my own childhood face: the Lía Margarita to whom this book is dedicated. The boy whose use of language brings laughter and awe. The boy who has solidarity running in his veins, writes poems, paints. The boy who dissects as he thinks. The child with the haunted face, tenderness struggling with hurt. The child who lies. Like one of my children lied. Like I lied.

Continuity: loss of continuity might be my greatest fear.

Not yet a loss I must add to my list.

Not yet.

Notes

A Few Words

1. The reference is to Adrienne Rich's poem "A Wild Patience Has Taken Me This Far," from her book of the same name: *A Wild Patience Has Taken Me This Far: Poems 1978–1981* (New York: Norton, 1993).

The American People

1. Unlike most citizens, at a particular moment in my life I took out citizenship in another country and, despite my protestations, was told I had lost my birth status as a result. After many years abroad, I came home in 1984 and was soon after ordered deported due to opinions I expressed in a number of my books. According to a clause in the 1952 McCarran-Walter Immigration and Nationality Act, these were deemed to be "against the good order and happiness of the United States." I was forced to fight to regain my citizenship, something I accomplished with a great deal of support almost five years later. (See my own *Coming Home: Peace without Complacency* [Albuquerque NM: West End Press, 1990], as well as works by others.) When I say I am a citizen,

it therefore means something quite a bit more complex and harder-won than the usual claim.

2. The stand-down at Fort Campbell was called after eleven suicides over a brief period of time were reported at the base. One hundred fifteen suicides were documented throughout the U.S. Army in 2007, with increasing numbers since. On October 24, 2010, ABC News reported 1,000 military suicides in the year. Among the incidents of troop-on-troop murder, the two most publicized cases took place at a stress clinic near Baghdad on May 13, 2009, when a soldier who had sought help at the clinic gunned down five military personnel; and at Fort Hood, Texas, on November 6, 2009, when an army psychiatrist murdered thirteen and wounded thirty. From reports by CNN, ABC, and other news sources.

Pumping Gas

1. According to the National Council on Radiation Protection and Measurement, *Discover Magazine*, May 2009, p. 14.

2. Inti Peredo led the Bolivian guerilla after Che Guevara's death in 1967. His brother Coco was also part of that effort. A younger brother, Chato, later rose in the ranks of that country's Movement toward Socialism and is today a member of Evo Morales's government.

3. Joan of Arc (1412–31) was a young French liberator burned at the stake when she defied the Church. When he wrote on the art of memory and infinity of the universe, the Italian philosopher Giordano Bruno (1548–1600) was put to death by the same medieval Church. Galileo (1564–1642) defied Church teaching by demonstrating that the sun and not the earth was the center of the universe. He was threatened with death and made to recant. Archbishop Oscar Romero (1917–80) followed liberation theology and sided with the poor during El Salvador's long rebel war; he was gunned down while saying mass. These are only a few in the long list of men and women throughout history who have been sacrificed by religious authoritarianism.

Race and Racism

1. Delivered on March 18, 2008, at Constitution Center, Philadelphia, Pennsylvania.

2. From ABC News as well as many other sources.

3. On September 15, 1963, at the height of the Civil Rights movement, Denise McNair, Cynthia Wesley, Carole Robertson, and Addie Mae Collins were killed by a bomb that exploded where they were attending Sunday School at the Sixteenth Street Baptist Church in Birmingham, Alabama. They were

between eleven and fourteen years of age. At the time it was impossible to bring the murderers to trial, and the FBI closed the case in 1968. It was reopened in the 1970s and, through the tenacious efforts of those who wanted to see justice served, four men were tried and ultimately convicted. One had already died. Three spent time in prison. According to those covering the case, the guilty continued to "wear their crime like a badge of honor."

4. A theory developed after polls predicted that a black man, Tom Bradley, would win the 1982 California governorship. When he didn't win, it was assumed that many of those polled had said they would vote for him but didn't because of his race.

5. According to a report on NPR, December 18, 2009, people of color will outnumber whites in the United States by 2050.

The Cell Remembers

1. Craig Childs, *The Secret Knowledge of Water* (Seattle: Sasquatch Books, 2000), pp. 61–62. Italics in the original.

2. Jennifer Barone, "Slime Molds Show Primitive Smarts," *Discover Magazine*, January 2009, p. 58.

3. Dr. Todd C. Sacktor and his team at SUNY Downstate Medical Center in Brooklyn are among a number of neuroscientists now working on memory. According to the Society for Neuroscience, in 2008 alone the National Institutes of Health spent $5.2 billion, nearly 20 percent of its total budget, on brain-related projects. From Benedict Carey, "Brain Researchers Open Door to Editing Memory," *New York Times*, April 6, 2009.

4. I worked with Becky Bosch, an Albuquerque therapist who practices Radix, based in part on the work of Wilhelm Reich. I write about the experience in my book *This Is about Incest* (Ithaca NY: Firebrand Books, 1987).

5. Margaret Randall, *When I Look into the Mirror and See You: Women, Terror, and Resistance* (New Brunswick NJ: Rutgers University Press, 2003).

6. *When I Look into the Mirror*, p. 54.

7. *When I Look into the Mirror*, p. 55.

8. Although there has been no viable movement in this direction here in the United States, as I write a Spanish court has accepted Judge Baltazar Garzón's petition to open a criminal case against six Bush administration officials. They are former attorney general Alberto Gonzáles; former under secretary of defense for policy Douglas Feith; former vice president Dick Cheney's chief of staff, David Addington; Justice Department officials John Yoo and Jay S. Bybee; and former Pentagon lawyer William Haynes. Unfortunately, it so far seems impossible to accuse the men at the top: Bush himself, Cheney, and

former secretary of defense Donald Rumsfeld, among others. Garzón is the well-known human rights judge who brought the case against Chilean dictator Augusto Pinochet. Whether or not these new cases prosper remains to be seen. At the very least, if the Spanish court agrees to hear them, these men will not be able to travel outside the United States for fear of being captured and made to stand trial (Associated Press, March 28, 2009).

9. *A Feeling for the Organism* (New York: W. H. Freeman and Co., 1983) is Evelyn Fox Keller's important book about McClintock's life and work. The phrase "incomprehensible, mystical, even mad," describing McClintock's colleague's initial response to her theories, is from p. 148.

Rolling Eyes

1. Joby Warrick, "Little Blue Pills among the Ways CIA Wins Friends in Afghanistan," *Washington Post*, December 26, 2008.

2. Vice President Dick Cheney described waterboarding in this way on U.S. TV on October 26, 2008.

3. Both published by Little Brown and Company, New York and Boston, 2005 and 2008 respectively.

First Laugh

1. The phallogocentric system of language (Laçan and others) is based on the idea of binary opposites: male/female, order/chaos, language/silence, light/dark, good/evil, etc. The first term is valued over the second. In today's more complex understanding of race and gender, this notion becomes increasingly useless.

Piercing the Walls

Based on the keynote for "Dueling Eagles: A Seminar on U.S.-Mexico Border Issues" at the University of Oklahoma, Norman, Oklahoma, November 2, 2009. Rewrite and expansion of an earlier talk given at Naropa University in Boulder, Colorado, in June 2008.

1. Chellis Glendinning, *Off the Map* (Gabriola Island, BC, Canada: New Society Publishers, 2002).

2. Edward Said, *Culture and Imperialism* (New York: Vintage, 1993), pp. 5–6.

3. "From Iron Curtain to Green Belt: How Life Came to the Death Strip" by Tony Paterson, *Independent*, May 17, 2009.

4. For a more detailed description of the Anta Project, go to www.soni canta.com. For articles on Friendship Park, between Tijuana and San Diego,

where Sunday communion took place before the Department of Homeland Security stopped the practice, see the NPR site (www.npr.org) for February 9, 2009, among other sources. The National Geographic and many individual photographers have published border images.

Oñate's Right Foot

Woven Stone by Simon Ortíz (Tucson: University of Arizona Press, 1992), p. 224. Reprinted by permission.

1. Indians were already living here, yet as with so many such situations, the city's "founding" is dated to the Spanish settlement in 1706. The 2006 anniversary gave rise to all sorts of publicity and money-making schemes. Would that the organizers had seen fit to point us toward some truthful history; but this was left to the protestors.

2. Conversation with author.

3. There has been strangely little published about the Pueblo Revolt and its immediate aftermath; and even among Indian scholars no real agreement about this chapter in their history. For one of the few overviews, see *The Pueblo Revolt* by David Roberts (New York: Simon and Schuster, 2004).

4. The prime mover of the Oñate statues has been the Hispanic Cultural Preservation League. Not all people of Hispanic descent are insensitive to the Indian genocide, but this committee clearly wields power and influence.

5. In 2005 a statue of Popé created by Jémez Pueblo artist Cliff Fragua was added to the group of one hundred statues of notable citizens—two from each state—installed in the National Statuary Hall in the nation's Capitol. No statue of Popé yet exists on his native land.

Can Poetry Matter?

Based on a presentation given at a panel that was part of the Stir Poetry Festival, Albuquerque, New Mexico, September 13, 2008. The panel was organized by the Albuquerque poet Lisa Gill, who titled it in honor of Dana Gioia's 1991 essay by the same name. An abridged version of this essay first appeared in *World Literature Today* 84.2 (March-April 2010): 20–22, and is reprinted here by permission.

1. The Vietnamese poet (1766–1820) whose epic "Tale of Kieu" millions recite by heart.

2. From Mary Oliver, *American Primitive* (Boston: Back Bay Books, 1983).

3. The Zona Rosa was a few square blocks in the city's Colonia Cuauhtemoc, frequented at the time by artists and writers.

4. The name of the journal referred to the jazz horn from the United States

and the plumes of Mexico's pre-Columbian Quetzalcoatl, symbolizing the important contributions of both cultures. *El Corno Emplumado: A History of the Sixties* is an excellent film now available on DVD.

5. First published in *Their Backs to the Sea: Poems and Photographs* (San Antonio TX: Wings Press, 2009). Reprinted by permission.

6. First published in Spanish in *España, Aparta de mí este cáliz* by César Vallejo in 1937. The translation here is my own and has never been published elsewhere.

Words for *El Corno Emplumado*
Contribution to a panel held at New York University's King Juan Carlos Center, September 29, 2006.

The Living Silence
Based on a talk given at the Latin American Studies Association Meeting (LASA), Las Vegas, Nevada, October 8, 2004. Although five years have passed and we now have a different political scenario with a different balance of power, our most serious problems remain substantially unchanged. For this reason I have decided to include this talk as I delivered it rather than update it in any major way.

1. Margaret Randall, *Gathering Rage: The Failure of 20th Century Revolutions to Develop a Feminist Agenda* (New York: Monthly Review Press, 1992).

2. Margaret Randall, *Sandino's Daughters Revisited: Feminism in Nicaragua* (New Brunswick NJ: Rutgers University Press, 1994).

3. Margaret Randall, *Las hijas de Sandino: Una historia abierta* (Managua, Nicaragua: Amana, 1999).

4. Margaret Randall, *When I Look into the Mirror and See You: Women, Terror, and Resistance* (New Brunswick NJ: Rutgers University Press, 2003).

5. Since delivering and revising this essay, I have published another book that goes even further in exploring these issues: *To Change the World: My Years in Cuba* (New Brunswick NJ: Rutgers University Press, 2009). This book—part memoir, part analysis—continues to deepen my contribution to our collective ongoing conversation about identity and social change.

6. Kiet Seel is one of three ruins managed by Navajo National Monument, under the joint auspices of the U.S. National Park Service and the Navajo Nation. Between late May and early September, the Monument allows twenty hikers a day to visit the site. Reservations must be made several months in advance, and attendance at an orientation meeting the day before the hike is required.

Betrayal

1. John Noble Wilford and Laurie Goodstein, "'Gospel of Judas' Surfaces after 1,700 Years," *New York Times*, April 6, 2006.

2. The councils of Jerusalem (50 AD), Nicea (325 AD), Constantinople (381 AD), Ephesus (431 and 439 AD), and Chalcedon (451 AD) were the most important of these. Debated were issues such as Mary's immaculate conception, the divinity of Jesus, the Holy Trinity, which versions of Jesus' life would be designated as authoritative, and much else.

3. The feminist cultural critic Susan Guber (*Judas: A Biography* [New York: W. W. Norton and Co., 2009]), among others, makes a strong case for the Judas parable as Jew hatred. She points out that the gospel writers gave the betrayer the name of Judas—that is, Yehuda, the name of Jacob's son and the Israelite kingdom, from which the word Judaism derives. See Adam Kirsch's review of Guber's *Judas*, in *New York Times Book Review*, April 5, 2009.

4. I am speaking here about Daniel Ortega, once a Sandinista leader and then president of Nicaragua, whose step-daughter, Zoilamérica Narváez, publicly accused him of having sexually abused her over a period of nineteen years. Zoilamérica's mother defended her husband rather than her daughter, and Ortega himself forbade discussion of the charge. Today he is once again president of Nicaragua, though at the head of a government that is in no way revolutionary.

5. Tessie Greenglass, Ethel and David's mother, visited Ethel in prison, urging her to testify against her husband, to forsake him in exchange for being allowed to go home to her two little boys. "You should have thought about your politics before having children," she is reported to have told her daughter. Ethel refused to betray her husband to save herself. Unknowingly, my own mother used almost exactly the same words with me, when I was forced underground in 1969 Mexico and asked her to take my children until I could secure a way out of that country. She refused, telling me I should have thought about my politics before having children or my children before becoming involved in radical politics. Fortunately, in my case the stakes were not nearly so high.

6. On *Sixty Minutes II*, December 5, 2001, apparently with neither satisfaction nor remorse.

7. Gubar, *Judas*. Jorge Luis Borges (Buenos Aires, Argentina, 1899–1986).

8. In spite of pressure by the executive branch, the *New York Times* and *Washington Post* both published the Papers. Censorship of the press has advanced to the point where this would be much more difficult today.

9. As this book goes to press, the so-called Wikileaks of close to 400,00 U.S.

military reports on the war in Iraq have surfaced. Will a different political time consider this revelation betrayal or necessary information?

Crystal's Gift
1. Major John Wesley Powell, the one-armed explorer and the first white man to row the entire Colorado River, on his second attempt in 1869.

The Place Where Color Sounds
1. *Untitled (Perfect Lovers)* (1991), by Felix González Torres, as seen at the Wadsworth Athenaeum in Hartford, Connecticut.
2. William Carlos Williams, Adrienne Rich, Joy Harjo: all ground-breaking poets writing in American English.
3. On the occasion of the fiftieth anniversary of the failed uprising against Chinese rule.

My Losses
1. A once-popular typeface designed by Grambattista Bodoni (1740–1813). Today it is considered too cluttered by some, but it was the type we used for *El Corno Emplumado* back in the 1960s.
2. A combination of three drugs—efavirenz, lamivudine, and zidovudine (AZT)—began attacking the virus and keeping those who could afford them healthy. Millions who once resigned themselves to death started living longer, much longer. For years many have even been asymptomatic. Recently, however, the cocktail's long-term effects have been noted. They aren't good: an apparent weakening of the heart and other ills.

Breinigsville, PA USA
05 January 2011
252683BV00002B/2/P